Growing Younger

Welcoming families into the local church

Roger Morgan

ReSource

ReSource – helping to build a church which is diverse, local, renewed in the Spirit and effective in mission

Published in the UK by ReSource
13 Sadler Street, Wells, Somerset BA5 2RR
www.resource-arm.net
office@resource-arm.net
Charity no. 327035

ISBN 978-1-906363-41-3

Acknowledgements

Image on p 1 © istockphoto.com
Church image © Hans-Jörg Nisch, reproduced under licence from Fotolia.com.

Typing by Paula Smit
Design and layout by Alison Morgan

Thanks are due to all those who have contributed their experience and expertise to the research and production of this book. Every effort has been made to ensure the accuracy of the examples given, and any errors of fact are ours alone.

Printed by Flexpress, 6 Coal Cart Rd, Birstall, Leicester LE4 3BY

CONTENTS

About the author

Canon Roger Morgan works for ReSource, an Anglican initiative formed in 2004 to support and resource the church in renewal and mission.

Roger's first career was as a mathematician and management consultant. He spent seventeen years as a lecturer and Director of Studies at Cambridge University, working in the Engineering Department and as a Fellow of Corpus Christi College. During this time he also became Head of the Management Studies department, and was widely commissioned as a management consultant to industry.

While in Cambridge Roger built up a ministry among both students and townspeople, and worked in partnership with Daniel Cozens of Through Faith Missions, planning and leading parish missions all over the country. Roger was ordained in 1981, and from 1984-2008 he served in full time parish ministry, first as vicar of St Columba's, Corby and then as vicar of Holy Trinity, Leicester. He was made an honorary Canon of Leicester Cathedral in 2006. During his time at Holy Trinity Roger built up a staff team of 10, planted a new church, developed a multimedia outreach programme, and established a network of cell groups involving over 650 people.

Roger joined the ReSource team in 2008. Within ReSource Roger focusses on mission and mentoring. He leads ReSource's clergy mentoring programme EQUIP, and offers support for evangelism through written resources, training events and parish missions. More recently he has been seeking to identify best practice for ministry to families within the local church, and this book is the result not just of his own experience but of wide-ranging consultation all over the UK.

ReSource is an independent charity based in Wells, Somerset. Our vision is to help build a church which is diverse, local, renewed in the Spirit and effective in mission. We work with local churches of all types and traditions, with deaneries, dioceses and other denominational groupings. Our patron is Archbishop John Sentamu.

ReSource
13 Sadler St, Wells, Somerset BA5 2RR
www.resource-arm.net
office@resource-arm.net

INTRODUCTION
FROM VISION TO REALITY

Vision

For six years in the 1980s I was vicar of St Columba's, Corby, in Northamptonshire; this was my first experience of leading a church. In many ways they were wonderful years. I learned so much from my congregation about the true meaning of love and of worship. It was in Corby that I first learned how a group of Christians could exercise the gifts of the Spirit together. I learned how to listen to people whose lives had been damaged by traumatic events, and then how to bring them to Christ for healing. In Corby we saw fifty new people come into the Kingdom of God. These were good years.

And yet as I look back I so wish that I could have my time there all over again. Why? Because I realise now that I could have done so much more for the children. What could have happened, and still could happen in Corby today, is the emergence of a growing company of children conspicuous for their joy, their love for God, their spiritual power, and the power of their lives to influence others. These children could have been at the centre of the church, which is where Jesus wants them. This could have happened, but it didn't. It didn't because it was never part of my vision to make it happen. In this respect Corby was a missed opportunity.

Every church leader, in whatever denomination, has this same opportunity. Donna Williams is the children's pastor at St John's, Hampton Wick in London. Four years ago, when she joined, the church had nine children in the congregation: some regulars, some less so. Today nine have become 147. Alex Scott has been the children's pastor at Holy Trinity Leicester for the last twelve years. Growth in Leicester has been less spectacular than in Hampton Wick but it has been steady. Holy Trinity now has hundreds of children involved. To meet with groups of children in these churches is to be immediately filled with hope for the future.

So how have Donna and Alex achieved this? Many factors of course, but one stands out; they have both set out to disciple their children.

This has meant having a high expectation of what God can do in and through children, and setting high standards of commitment, behaviour, and faith. Alex has observed that at the age of nine most churchgoing children make a decision either to spend the rest of their lives following Jesus, or to give up belonging to the church as soon as they can square this with their parents. Alex often works with children from birth, which means he has nine years to reveal God to them and ensure that they go the right way. So like Donna, he has a very ambitious programme. For Alex and for Donna it is not enough to tell the children a Bible story and give them some colouring books.

Many churches, if they have any children at all, do what I did in Corby and concentrate on the adults. Then, because some of those adults have children, the children are cared for in the context of the Sunday worship, though they never become the focus. But when children do become the focus, you can expect to see spectacular growth. And because the children are the future you can expect through them to transform the future of our society. There is no other obvious way for the church to do this.

Imagine a church in which you have children like these, all real children, all aged between four and ten:

- John believes that his life has been created by God for a specific purpose. John can't wait to discover what that purpose is, and this affects everything he does.

- Sam's father died when he was eight. At first Sam was very angry with God but then Sam decided to put his future in God's hands and to trust him. As a result Sam's intimacy with his heavenly father is growing daily.

- Katie went with the Sunday Club on a weekend away. There she heard the gospel explained and she became a Christian. She invited Jesus into her life and he has become her friend.

- Jason stole some stuff at school and got into trouble for it. Then at church he heard how Jesus had died so that he might be forgiven. Jason received forgiveness for his sins and the experience has changed him. He doesn't need to steal things any more.

- Polly heard about the Holy Spirit and she asked Jesus to fill her. The encounter with God that followed is something she often talks about.

- Simon woke up in the middle of the night and found that God was speaking to him. He knew that his mother was going to have another baby and that he must do all that he could to help her when the baby came.

- On Sundays Jenny looks forward to communion. Usually the children rejoin their parents at the end of the service; Jenny is not allowed to take the wine but she receives the bread with great seriousness. Every week she takes into herself the Bread of life, and Jesus is being formed in her heart.

- Billy likes talking to God. He learned to do this at Sunday Club and found that when he tried speaking his prayers out loud God seemed very close to him.

- Susan has learned that God answers her prayers. When she wants something either for herself or others, she always asks God if it is okay to pray. If the answer is 'yes' then she goes ahead. Susan's faith is growing.

- Philip goes to a school where success in the exams is everything. But Philip listened to what they said at Sunday Club about work being a way of glorifying God, so now he does his work to please God and not please the teachers. The stress has gone and Philip is enjoying his work.

- At Emma's school all the girls have best friends, but Emma has no one. At church Emma learned that everyone matters to God so she has decided that everyone will matter to her, even the people who tease her or ignore her. As a result Emma has become one of the most popular girls in her group.

- Alfie has prayed for his friends and invites them to church at every opportunity. One of his friends has become a Christian and is doing well.

- Clare learned at church that the Holy Spirit can give power to heal.

She asked for this power and she started to pray for her friends when they were sick. One day one of her friends was healed through her prayers.

- Ed's hamster died. Ed and his mother held the stiff hamster and prayed; as they prayed bit by bit the hamster came to life.

- Alice decided to tithe her pocket money. Since she did this she has discovered that she is never short of money.

- Emily has adopted an African girl from a poor family. Every month she sends money and writes; as a result the African girl is able to go to school.

- Frankie has decided to commit scripture to memory and he has memorised twenty promises from the Bible. Day by day he lives by those promises.

- Ellie sets her alarm and gets up every day to pray and read her Bible. She is very confident now that her heavenly father loves her and is with her every day. In her quiet times Ellie often hears God speaking to her.

- George was having serious doubts about God. Did God even exist? George shared his doubts with the Sunday Club teachers and they helped him to face them. Now George is beginning to know what he believes and why.

- Anne decided to get baptised by full immersion. All her friends came to the service. Anne feels like a new person.

- At Sunday Club Ruth is often asked to give short talks from the Bible. She is growing in skill and is much appreciated by the others.

- For Andy the best thing about being a Christian is the opportunity to worship God. He is learning the guitar and becoming a good worship leader. The other children love it when Andy leads.

These are real children, fruits of Donna's work in Hampton Wick and Alex's work in Leicester. I am telling their stories so that you can ponder what could happen to the children who live in your community if you tried to have a ministry among them.

Barham Downs

Over the last few years I have visited many churches; what I notice as I travel around is that most are not big and successful like Alex's or Donna's churches, and most cannot find people to lead of their calibre. But what I have seen and been heartened by is lots and lots of small success stories, often in quite small places.

One such story comes from Lesley Hardy and the Barham Downs benefice. Barham is a village near Canterbury with only five hundred homes. The hand of God is discernible in this story, but I couldn't help thinking that what has happened in Barham could be repeated, God willing, in any village of a similar size.

Stephen and Lesley arrived in Barham in 2009. At the time the church attendance averaged 35 a week, with mostly older people. The monthly family service was only slightly different in style from the other services. But there was one huge sign of hope. The family service was already being attended by three families. God had provided a team!

One thing that distinguishes Lesley is her ability to listen. She visited the three families straight away, and invited them to the vicarage for a meeting at which they all agreed to meet to pray together regularly. Lesley had previously run a Messy Church, and the prayer meeting agreed to offer one of these on a Sunday afternoon. Sixty people came including several dads.

Lesley noticed that some mums enjoyed the quiet bits of Messy Church, and proposed a quiet day; this led on to a weekly Bible study and prayer time to which toddlers were welcome. So now eight people were meeting regularly for fellowship – huge progress in just eighteen months.

Then at Christmas they introduced 'Messy Christmas', a one-off amalgam of Messy Church and the family service. This drew 150 people, which encouraged them to start quarterly Café Church on Sundays, beginning with breakfast. Café Church sees around 100 people coming every time. It helped that God provided a really good guitarist just when this was needed.

Meanwhile the monthly family service has been redesigned to make it family friendly. Four years on, 50 adults and 25 children is the normal attendance. I think we should all be as encouraged and excited by this story as we are about well known success stories like Holy Trinity Brompton.

Reality

What Alex has achieved in Leicester and Donna in Hampton Wick is not typical of the churches in England today. Neither is the church in Barham typical.

To help you understand what is really going on in most of our churches, I would like to introduce you to Mark. About a year ago I went to his induction service as a new Church of England vicar. Mark and his wife Rebecca are good friends of mine. They have two young children.

The service was inspiring, as these services usually are; full of purpose and hope. I left feeling as I always do, and as I think I am supposed to. We had been told by the Bishop that Mark and Rebecca have a job to do and that with the help of God they will be able to get it done. The service made it clear what that job is: they are to minister to their congregations (they have two), and band their people together to share the love of God and the message of Jesus with all those who live in their parishes. This includes hundreds of children, almost all of whom are completely unchurched.

An inspiring evening, but in the cold light of the next day the task did not look quite so easy. The starting point was not good. The congregations Mark and Rebecca had come to serve were small in number and the people were mostly elderly; the family's arrival had raised the number of children present from two to four. I realised that unless Mark did something radical his people would simply grow old and die, leaving behind only an empty building.

So I left the induction service wishing that I could do something to encourage Mark and Rebecca and fill them with hope for the future. I tried to put myself in their shoes and asked myself how I would go about their task if it was mine. The result is this book; I am deliberately writing not for people like Donna and Alex, but for people like Mark and Rebecca.

The Basic Questions

Thinking about Mark's task and the task of many like him causes me to ask the following basic questions. Having asked these questions I will spend the rest of the book trying to answer them. The questions are these:

The first question: How can a church with very few children become a church with lots of children? Putting it another way, what is the ten year plan that would take a church from point A to point B?

A. The wider community in which the church is set has people of all ages, but the church community is mostly aged over fifty.

B. The church community reflects the wider community; more than 20% of the church community are aged under eighteen.

To move from A to B what should someone like Mark do as a first step? And what next, and so on...?

The second question: How can a church which does have children best nurture those children so as to ensure that most of them enter adult life as disciples of Jesus?

To try to answer these questions I decided to do some research, and I began with my friend David Keen. I invited David to give his answer to these basic questions, confining himself to one side of paper. I then circulated David's answer around the excellent ReSource network; about 150 people responded, some at considerable length, and including some who clearly have weighty experience. Then I wrote the first draft of this book, circulated it as widely as I could, and received more valuable responses. I also paid a number of visits to people who seemed to have a story to tell, and I have included many of these stories in this book.

I feel that I have seen enough now to be able to discern the outline of a way forward. As a result of my researches I now know what my plan of action would be should I ever again be in Mark's shoes. And I have seen a few places where something like this plan is being followed with encouraging results.

My hope will be to produce an update to this book before too long, perhaps within two or three years. In the meantime I would like to hear from you. Some of you I am sure will have stories to tell, and others I am equally sure will have fresh ideas from which we can all learn. The aim is to start a movement of people who are determined to build churches in which the children of this generation will come to know and serve Jesus in ever increasing numbers. Can this be done? I believe it can!

Roger Morgan
Wells, February 2015

ESSENTIAL NOTE: Safeguarding children

It is the responsibility of every local church to create a safe environment for children and their families. All work with children should be conducted within the appropriate safeguarding guidelines laid down by every diocese or denomination. This will normally mean that all those who work directly with children should hold a current Disclosure and Barring Service (DBS) certificate. More information is provided by the following organisations:

The Churches' Agency for Safeguarding: www.churchsafe.org.uk
The Church of England Safeguarding Statements and Practice Guidance: www.churchofengland.org.uk.

1. START FROM WHERE YOU ARE

Mark and Rebecca are getting their first taste of church leadership in a small town in central England. The churches they serve are typical in that there are few children involved. Mark and Rebecca have children of their own, and if only for the sake of their own family this situation cannot continue.

So how should Mark and Rebecca get started? What should occupy their minds and time in the first months? I have thought about this in many contexts now, and have little doubt about the answer. The place to start is not with children at all; not with any new projects but with the existing congregations. Always start from where you are.

I have observed some clergy (myself included!) who, discouraged by the lack of enthusiasm of the existing church members, quickly initiate new projects and absorb themselves in them whilst at the same time enduring what they fear cannot be changed. What I notice is that there is always a price to pay for this approach; experience suggests that it is better to first work and pray for the renewal of what is already there. This is also I think what Mark promised to do at his induction service. Mark and Rebecca should give their hearts, their time, their prayers and their love to the people who are already there, seeing and believing in their potential. Later on they will be repaid for this patient approach.

All over the country there are church congregations, and it is in these congregations that God has placed his Spirit. A church of just five elderly people is a church with Jesus in the midst. It may already be experiencing life, love and power. These things are attractive and this church will bear fruit. These are the assumptions with which Mark and Rebecca should begin.

And yet it is also true that they may find, when they get to know them, that their two congregations are, spiritually speaking, almost lifeless. There may be no one for Mark and Rebecca to pray with, no one who will love them, no one who will bring them a word from the Lord. If this is what they find, then they must preach to them as Jonah preached to Nineveh.

They must tell them the story of Jesus, lead them one by one to repentance and faith, and pray that spiritual life will flow into them and among them. And as Mark and Rebecca preach to them and pray for them, then in a host of different ways they must also demonstrate that they love them.

And perhaps one day they will reach the point where they can say 'we now have a spiritual church. These people love God, they love their Bibles, they love to worship, they love to pray together. Our people love each other, they love their neighbours, and they are in touch with the power of God. When newcomers try out the services they may not find people of their own age and type, but they do find something which attracts them and holds them; this something is the presence of Jesus.' A time will come when Mark's church is no longer just a religious club; it is a community of disciples.

In the Introduction I introduced you to two successful children's workers, Donna from Hampton Wick and Alex from Leicester. Donna and Alex work with children in the context of two very healthy churches, churches that are full of life and faith, joy and power. Children's work flourishes best in churches like these. Of course Mark and Rebecca may find that they already have a congregation similar to the ones which Donna and Alex originally joined. But I doubt it. At the point where Mark takes over, his churches are outwardly failing, and that is probably symptomatic of an inner failure. So Mark and Rebecca probably have a lot of remedial work and a lot of praying to do.

Some readers may like to turn now to the Appendix on p124. There I outline the steps that someone like Mark must take in order to turn a church which is not functioning well into one that is. If you feel that your church is already in a good place, there will be no need to read this appendix; but if not maybe you should look at it now. To reiterate my point: if your church is not in a good place, do not put your energy into new projects; first sort out your church.

Cambridgeshire - an example of how to begin

Throughout this book I will give examples of good practice that I have discovered on my travels. I began with Hampton Wick, Leicester and Barham. The next story comes from Anne Shorter, who has been vicar of a traditional Anglican church in Cambridgeshire for just nine months. She arrived to find a congregation small in number, mostly very elderly, and full of conflicts that had not been handled well. Hurt feelings were running deep.

Anne did not rush out to try to recruit new and younger people; instead she sent out personal invitations to a meeting of the existing congregation. Most came, and Anne invited them each to share along the following lines:

- How did you come to be part of this church?
- Is there a particular spiritual memory that sustains you?
- Can you recall a time when you met God in a life-changing way?

This meeting proved to be the beginning of a breakthrough. Those who came spoke with enthusiasm and animation about things some had never shared before. Then one very elderly man stood up and said, "About thirty years ago my wife was almost paralysed by arthritis. We saw an advertisement for a Christian healing service in a nearby church. The leader invited any who would like prayer to come forward, and I carried her up to the rail. After prayer, she walked out by herself. The following day she was working in the garden for the first time in years."

Anne writes, 'There followed one of those holy moments when each of us knew that God was with us. Since then I have prayed the Eucharistic Prayer, "The Lord is here", with great confidence because I really know that "His Spirit **is** with us." The current congregation now supports Anne's policy of working closely with the local school, and later this year they will be starting an all age service.

Warnings

As you read this book you will see that from time to time I will flag up potential mistakes – sometimes ones I have made myself, sometimes ones I have seen others make. This is the first one:

> Warning: A new incumbent or minister should not despair of the congregation he or she finds. Never stop believing that your church, however much it is struggling outwardly, is actually the temple of the Holy Spirit. Anticipate from the beginning that you will be able to build a great church starting with these people.

And this is this is the second warning. I have seen this happen with serious consequences for the person involved:

> Warning: If your church has very little spiritual life do not try to solve your problems by recruiting a paid family worker, even if you have the money. Building a work among children and families is tough, and if the person you bring in is not part of a good church, he or she is likely to die spiritually. So sort your church out first.

2. TIME FOR SOMETHING NEW

I spent 24 years in parish ministry, serving first in Corby and then in Leicester. Happily the two churches that I moved to were much further forward than the ones Mark and Rebecca have found. Many of the steps which I outline in the Appendix had already been taken by my predecessors; and both churches had plenty of life.

Even so I was to find, as most do, that the early years of my ministry in these places were not the best ones. Generally speaking it is in the early years that foundational or even repair work has to be done; even small changes can result in big conflicts. The best years come when fresh vision appears, when everyone pursues that vision together, and God blesses it.

> **Warning: The early years of a new ministry can be difficult; they are a time to be patient. But they are not a time to give up, they are a time to have faith. Many have come through tough times and gone on to see remarkable church growth.**

So imagine Mark during his first months and years in the new parish, the hard years when he is laying foundations for the future. Imagine him working away at his existing congregations; preaching, administering the sacraments, praying for people, caring for them, discipling them, facing up to conflicts, turning them bit by bit into a functioning church. This work will be the first priority for Mark's time.

But at the same time imagine him getting to know the wider parish, connecting with all aspects of life in the secular community, and especially with the schools. These personal contacts matter. During this first phase, when Mark is focussing mainly on the church community, there will be little to show from the community links in terms of church attendance; but when the time comes for Mark and Rebecca to do something new and to focus their attention on building a ministry to families, the reputation that they have already established in the secular community will count for a lot.

And as you imagine Mark strengthening the churches and making links in the community, imagine Mark and Rebecca at their prayers – prayers which God is guiding, prayers which are stirring their hearts to love the wider community as well as the church people. At first it is only Mark and Rebecca who are praying, but soon there are others who are praying with them. The church is beginning to care about the community and is listening to God for direction.

> **Warning: A new church leader should strike out for fresh vision only when God indicates that the time is right. Pray first. Pray fervently. Find others to pray with you.**

At a moment of God's choosing will come a time for decision, a time to do something new. When this moment comes Mark and Rebecca will need a plan, a plan to change their church. In this book I will describe this plan as a series of steps. The first step will be to get everyone talking and praying about the new vision – a vision for a younger church, a church which has lots of children.

3. LISTEN TO PEOPLE AND TO GOD

As I write this a cabinet minister has just been sacked. A lot of people are amazed because he has been a man with many brilliant and original ideas, and the types of reform he wanted are desperately needed. So why has he been sacked? I suspect it is because, although he is undoubtedly a good talker, he has not been a good listener. This man had vision, but because he hasn't been listening his vision is not shared by many of the key players. So they have removed him.

Like this cabinet minister I have always enjoyed analysing problems and coming up with solutions, and I mistakenly thought that this is what good leadership consists of. Actually it isn't – indeed in the early stages of my ministry I found that my analytical skills were more of a handicap than a help. Rather than offering solutions, Mark will find that the listening approach works better; the approach that assumes that other people may have better ideas and solutions than he does – sometimes the most surprising people, sometimes even quite awkward people!

The truth is that every single person in Mark's church community, and most people in the secular community, already know what the problem is. They know full well that the church is losing touch with the younger generation; they also mostly agree that this is a bad thing and that something should be done about it. If Mark wants to help the church grow younger he will find masses of goodwill everywhere he goes.

But more than that, not only do the people in the two communities, church and parish, know what the problem is, they also, between them, know what the solution is. If you don't believe me, watch David Dimbleby's Question Time on a Thursday evening. You will see that the ideas of the people in the audience are often better than the ideas of the experts on the panel.

> **Warning: If you are planning a major change of direction do not move too quickly. Take your time and include as many people as possible in the discussions leading up to the change. And trust people. Most of those who do not welcome your ideas are not against you; they are merely fearful or cautious. Some of what they say may even be right!**

So Mark's first task is to hear what everyone else thinks. Mark and Rebecca should have conversations with one person after another, taking every opportunity. Mark will probably want to listen first to his elders or wardens and then to the church council, but his aim should be to include everyone in the discussions. He should also invite someone who has experience of working with younger people to talk at a meeting to which everyone in the two congregations is invited. At this stage the vision can be expressed in quite broad terms. 'We must do something to welcome younger people, including families; do you agree? And if you do, what ideas do you have?' Mark should say this to everyone in his congregations and to everyone he meets in the community.

As they listen Mark and Rebecca will find that people are mostly very positive and that some have good ideas. Some of these will perhaps be people who are not yet part of the church community. Mark will find that, as he begins to talk vision, interested people will appear from surprising places. These enthusiasts will be very important later when assembling teams and formulating plans.

Mark may also find that he runs into some who tell him it has all been tried before and can't be done. If he does he must not be surprised or lose courage. People need to express themselves; some people are naturally conservative, with an instinctive fear of any kind of change. Mark should keep listening, always confident that God is with him and that he will succeed in the end. If he listens respectfully to the negative voices he will find that some of these people will eventually become his greatest allies.

> **Warning: Listen to what people have to say but at this stage do not take any votes; votes polarise people. There will be time to vote later when Mark has a firm proposal to put on the table.**

As well as listening to people, Mark should do his best to listen to God. And at this time of change it will be important to get his church members praying as well as talking. In my own ministry I found that when I raised an issue at a church council meeting the advice given could be very helpful; but when I raised the same issue at a prayer meeting the insights

I gained were usually even more helpful. And sometimes, as we listened to God together, we were all of us given the sense that we had received very clear guidance about the way we should go.

> **Warning: Before you go ahead with fresh vision call people together to pray and listen to God. The right time to go forward is when you have a sense that God has spoken.**

4. DECIDE ON A LEADER

The message of the last chapter was that, in the search for fresh vision, consensus works much better than dictatorship. So before leading your church in a new direction it is important to hear the views of as many people as possible. But after that, if you want to get things done, don't form a committee or hold a vote: put someone in charge and make that person accountable. Find one person, or two at the most, to take overall responsibility.

> **Warning: Never put the leadership of a new ministry into the hands of a committee. Put one person in charge (at most two) and make them accountable to the church leader.**

> **Warning: Do not hesitate to make a change in the leadership of the children's ministry if this is necessary. In some churches there are people who have been leading the work for a long time. If you have confidence in them that's fine; if not, you must find someone new. But be careful how you go about it: take your time, be as gentle as you can, honour the person as much as possible.**

Mark has a crucial decision to make. Will it work best for Mark himself to be the leader of the new work, or is somebody else going to do it? And if someone else is going to do it, will it be someone from the congregation working unpaid, or someone the church will pay?

Larger churches

Large churches will handle this differently from small churches. A large church which wants to develop a new area of ministry must be prepared to take on an additional paid staff member. Leaders who attempt to grow a bigger and bigger church without recruiting extra staff always suffer badly from overload and usually fail.

As a rough guide churches (or benefices) which already have 100 committed members should be asked to raise money to enable a new worker to be recruited, probably a family and children's worker. This post could be full or part time (I have found that two thirds often works well).

The new recruit, perhaps after an initial period of training, will become the leader of the new ministry to younger people. An alternative, which seems in practice to happen only rarely, is for the church leader to take on the new ministry while bringing in a new person to take some of the leader's existing load.

Warning: If the church is large do not introduce ambitious fresh vision without recruiting a new staff member.

If there is to be a new paid worker there will be significant financial implications. The church leader will need a well worked out proposal to put to the church council, to the church as a whole, or to whichever body takes the financial decisions. This proposal must explain why a new person is needed, what the job description will be, how much the new person will cost, and how if the person is successful it will lead to church growth and eventually to an increase in income.

A labourer is worthy of his or her hire; so always aim to pay what the person you appoint seems to be worth. For example if, as I once did, you decide to recruit a school teacher to your new church job, then pay roughly the same salary as a school would pay. It is almost always a mistake to pay a new person badly.

Warning: When you recruit a new staff member, recruit the best person you can find. Don't worry that this is expensive; plan to pay the new person every penny they are worth. That way you will get someone good who will stay in the job.

The proposal to recruit a new person should include ways of raising the money. Here are three possible ways:

- Obtain a grant to finance the new worker. In the Church of England some dioceses have special funds for this kind of appointment.

- Go directly to people you know to be wealthy, and ask them for funds to finance the first two years of the project on the understanding that the church will pick up the cost after that. Always ask them in person, explain why you need their help, and ask for a specific amount. Remember that wealthy people will normally give only if you ask them for a significant sum.

- Go to the church as a whole and hold a gift day. Ask people to give you enough money to fund the first two years. Don't say how much you are hoping they will give individually, but do let them know what the target figure is for the church as a whole. Emphasise that small gifts are valued greatly.

  Warning: Do not hesitate to go directly to wealthy Christians and ask them to give you their money. This may well be their best way to contribute to the kingdom. Take such people into your confidence; share your vision and let them know how they could help you. Remember that £1000 may seem a lot to you but it does not feel the same to someone who has much more than you have.

Do not go to the church council or church meeting with a proposal to raise money from the congregation unless you are confident that they will agree to it. So sound people out one at a time. Share your vision. Tell them how you hope to transform the church. Find out how each one is thinking. Ask them to pray. Answer their questions.

Sometimes a church will not agree to finance a new worker until they can see a demonstration that the new ministry is likely to produce results. So even when you are convinced that a new recruit is necessary, it may be better to get things started without one, putting the leadership in the hands of a volunteer or doing it yourself. When the church sees evidence of growth they will probably be ready to contemplate voting for funds to develop the new project further.

> **Warning: Raising and spending money is a tricky issue in a church and it is important to get wide agreement. So if you need to raise money take your time with people and be patient.**

Relying solely on advertising is risky; I know from both experience and research that 50% of people recruited by advertising and interview alone turn out to be the wrong people. So if there is to be a new paid worker, it may be best to appoint from the existing congregation, or, if not from the congregation, to choose someone already known to you – it is always wise to headhunt as well as to advertise. It is also important to speak to referees personally as well as reading what they write about an applicant.

When it comes to the interview, look for evidence that the person you are considering has a passion for children, with stories to tell about children they have worked with who have become disciples of Jesus. Ask yourself too whether this applicant would fit naturally with the culture of your church, and not be at odds with the way you do things and with the principles you stand for.

The new work will not be easy, so explore the candidate's previous experience of setbacks and assure yourself that when these come the person will be able to handle them. The new worker will need the ability to recruit others to work alongside them, so ask yourself if this person has qualities which will draw others to work with them. And always look for someone who is teachable and who has learned the principle of submission to leadership.

> **Warning: Be aware that it is easy to recruit the wrong person and as a result set the work back by several years. When recruiting take your time and be very careful.**

When the new paid worker starts he or she must be given a lot of the church leader's time in the first couple of years. This time commitment should continue until the two are of one mind about the vision and the leader is sure that the new person has the skills to get the job done without close supervision. The same applies if the leader decides to put the new ministry into the hands of a volunteer; be prepared to work very closely with that volunteer in the early years.

> **Warning: Do not recruit a new staff member and then just leave them to it. Work alongside the new person so that you can communicate your vision and give training as appropriate. Leave them to it only when they are fully envisioned and trained, and the relationship between you has become strong.**

Smaller churches

Churches (or benefices) with fewer than 100 will probably not be able to afford a new worker; so in a small church like Mark's the minister must either lead the new work himself or find a volunteer.

There might be a really good person available, and in Mark's case Rebecca would be an excellent choice if she is willing. But usually a volunteer will only be able to give a limited amount of time, and in the end this will limit the size of the ministry. Given the importance of this new work, Mark is probably best to take it on himself. This will require courage; a congregation of thirty or forty people aged over sixty often carry strong expectations for how the incumbent will use his or her time. If Mark is going to take this new ministry on himself it will take a *lot* of time – up to 50% of his total time – and this will no longer be available for other things.

> **Warning: If a church has a majority of people in their sixties and very few families, do not make the mistake of putting the ministry to families into the hands of a volunteer. To get significant change you must be prepared to take on the ministry yourself and put a great deal of time into it.**

If Mark is going to take the lead himself he should consider the possibility of trying to recruit an intern, someone who could act as his personal assistant and might also contribute towards the children's ministry. Interns are young people who come for a gap year, maybe two, not to lead the ministry but rather to work alongside the ministry leaders. In my own churches interns were accommodated free of charge by someone from the congregation. They were also given a personal pastor, usually an older person from the congregation, who acted both as a parent figure and as a spiritual guide. Employing interns need not be expensive, and many of our interns gave far more to us than they received from us.

It's best to headhunt for interns, using your contacts. Only bring in people who are highly recommended by someone you trust. The world is full of inspiring young people; why not get some of them working for you for a year or two?

5. FORM A CORE TEAM

Next we come to the most important step of all, but one which is so often left out. The leader of the new ministry, be that Mark himself or someone else, should not work alone but should put the highest priority possible on recruiting a team of sufficient size and quality to get the job done. 'Recruit the team then start the work' – not the other way round, as so often happens.

In one sense the whole church will be the team, because everyone in the church will have a part to play in supporting the new ministry; but what you are looking for now is a small number of people who will choose to commit a lot of time in the years ahead, and for whom the new ministry will become an absorbing and exciting journey.

These people will form what I call the core team. When the new ministry is launched the core team can always be augmented by others who can only offer limited time. For example someone might be willing to support the team by providing refreshments whenever there is an event, while someone else is willing to help with a children's club but only on a monthly basis. Such people are useful and very welcome but they should not to be regarded as part of the core team. The people in the core team need to be serious and committed, able to be there almost every week, strongly motivated by the vision and by the many opportunities they will have to work with people.

Mark, or Mark and his team leader, should be cautious about launching into a new ministry until this core team is of sufficient size and commitment. It may take a long time to get the team together, but it will be time well spent. At this stage the key issue is this: a team leader, once appointed, *should give the priority of their time not to ministry but to recruiting team members*. And even when things are up and running, large chunks of the team leader's time should go on increasing the size of the team and refreshing its members. Having a good team is everything.

> **Warning: Do not make the common mistake of starting an ambitious new ministry with an inadequate team. Instead postpone the launch of the ministry and use your time and**

energy to recruit a good team and to build vision and team spirit.

Jesus went up a mountain to pray; when he came down he called twelve people to be with him. These twelve became his core team. Jesus set high standards for his team; Mark and his team leader will also have to issue some challenges. People who already have six other church jobs will have to give some of them up. People who have huge work commitments will not be able to help. When you challenge people, challenge them to capacity. It's important not to over-challenge; people can only give what they have. But don't under-challenge either; ask for all that they can reasonably give, plus a bit more.

When Jesus left the earth he left behind some special people, people who had been on his team, people like Peter and John. When Mark leaves the parish he too must hope to leave behind people who have come to know God at a deep level and have discovered how to access God's power; people who will serve God for the rest of their lives. He will be able to do this only if he understands the importance of working with teams. Being on team and accepting team disciplines is where you learn: learn to pray, to commit, to sacrifice, to believe, to be humble and yet powerful. In his time Mark will need many teams – but for some the right team will be this one, the team that works with children and families.

The way for Mark to recruit a team is to do what Jesus did – throw himself into making contact with people, and then keep his eyes open. When he sees someone he wants on his team, he should ask them. He should say why he wants them and what will be involved. The worst that can happen is that they say no; but it is actually much easier to recruit a team than you might think. Many people are longing to do something useful with their lives; being on Mark's team may be just what they need to find fulfilment. But only ask people if you can see that they will have something important to offer.

Mark should also remember that people are much more likely to join him if they are impressed by him. Jesus was a man of vision with a clear understanding of what his mission was. Jesus also performed miracles, and the people who saw his miracles were the ones who wanted to join his team. Mark should be heard repeatedly sharing his vision and his confidence that God will enable him to grow the church by bringing in younger people. Mark should also let God be seen in his ministry, through his preaching, by the way that he prays, and through the way that he deals with people.

Mark and his team leader should make sure they have some youngish men in the team as well as women, and should not be afraid to have teenagers. I know of one parish just like Mark's where the incumbent seems oblivious to the fact that he has two fourteen year old boys who would commit ideas and energy if only he would let them. Leadership is not just for the over sixties!

> **Warning: When choosing a team do not fail to use your imagination; the obvious people are rarely the right people. Regard everyone you meet as a potential team member and listen for God's guidance.**

During my researches for this book I was asked to select a team for one particular church. I was told that there were a few older women who might be available if I approached them. I didn't do this. What I did do was run some family services and pay a visit to the local school. I noticed two people in particular. One was a fourteen year old boy who, after church, was busily engaged in a football game with some younger boys. The other was the school head who is full of the love of Jesus and has a heart of compassion for children. I thought these were both marvellous people so I asked them and was delighted when they agreed to join my team. No one that I asked said no. My eventual team had eight people: the head teacher, two teenagers, a single man with a gift for music, and four parents, two dads and two mums. This team has the right composition to reach out to families; we are now getting on with it and it is going well.

When selecting a team set high standards, and only choose FAT people – people who are Faithful, Available, and Teachable. Don't ask people who are not FAT – you will only have to ease them out later, and that is liable to be painful.

Warning: Team building is a matter of faith. You have to believe that if God has called you to this ministry he will also provide you with a team. Trust him. Do not get trapped by the false idea that your church is short of resources.

How big should the team be? There is no upper limit, and as the months go by Mark should aim to add new members. But to calculate a minimum, work out how many church members you have who are aged over thirty. Then divide this by eight to arrive at your minimum core team size. Mark's churches have sixty members between them, so he will need a team of about seven, including the team leader. A smaller number than this will not be able to build up a family ministry of sufficient size. These seven people will be necessary to recruit the twenty children or so that Mark will need to transform the character of the church, to nurture these children properly, and to reach out in friendship and with the gospel to their families. Getting and keeping the twenty children and their families will be hard work, and it may take some time, but with a team of seven it is a realistic target.

Warning: Do not finalise your team until it has at least one third of male members and two thirds that are aged under 55.

6. A SHORT PERIOD OF RESEARCH AND EXPERIMENTATION

I have often found inspiration in the story of Nehemiah and the wall which he built around Jerusalem. I notice that when he arrived in Jerusalem Nehemiah did not immediately start building; instead he took a few people with him and made a careful survey of the problem. Mark should follow Nehemiah's example. As the next step Mark and his team should engage in a short period of research.

> **Warning: Do not leap into starting a new programme without first having a proper period of research and experimentation. When you start something you need to know that it is likely to succeed. But do not let this period of research go on for too long. It is a question of balance; everyone will be hoping and expecting that something new will start to happen quite soon.**

First Mark's team should have a careful look at the parish itself. What else is happening for children and young people in the neighbourhood? Where are the schools and who has contact with them? Is anything else being done for young people? When do these other activities happen, and how popular are they?

They should also try to learn as much as they can from outside the parish. This means reading books, paying visits to other places, and exploring the internet. Are there churches in similar places which are making good progress, and what may be learned from them?

Next Mark and the team should try to make contact with the children who are living around them, and also with their parents. What are these people like? Are they busy or are they at a loose end? Are they happy or unhappy? What kinds of music do they like? What kinds of meetings or activities are they used to? The team should make friends wherever they can. They should be of any help they can. They should listen carefully. They should ask advice, being honest with people about what the church is trying to do.

Mark's aim is clear; he wants to involve the younger people in his patch in what he is doing. If they are in trouble, he wants to help them. If they are not yet Christians, he wants to make friends with them and share the gospel with them. If they are Christians, he wants to build them into a worshipping community. As Mark and the team get to know the children and young people in their area they will start to form plans. They will hope to be in a position to put together a programme which these young people will be keen to engage with.

In designing this programme Mark may find that many of his assumptions are challenged. For example, churches do not have to meet on Sunday morning; meetings do not have to consist of Common Worship services; you do not have to meet in a church building; you do not need to use an organ for your worship. If Sunday services with an organ held in the church building and using formal liturgy is going to help, then all well and good, but if not then Mark must find another way. This period of research is there to help him discover what that other way is.

This is also the time for Mark and his team to experiment. For example if Mark is minded to run a monthly family service, his team could try just doing one event to see how it goes. But at this stage they should be careful to avoid any regular commitments. That can come later when they know what is likely to work.

> **Warning: In designing a new programme be prepared to make really radical changes; there is no need to make change for change's sake, but do not assume that things must be as they have always been.**

Oakington

James Alexander is the vicar of Oakington, a village near Cambridge. The church is strong but, despite the excellent church school, only four Oakington families are presently linked to the church. James, with the agreement of his PCC, has decided to put the leadership of the family work into the hands of two

lay people, Nicola and Pete, both of whom have young children themselves. Nicola and Pete have begun to recruit a team and they are beginning to take soundings in the village. Nicola chose ten unchurched families and approached them, asking how the church could best serve their families. She found that nine out of the ten were positive about their family getting involved with the church.

Nicola and Pete remain flexible about the future shape of the ministry, but they are beginning to think that what they will want is a monthly event, probably on Sunday morning, aimed at families; a Sunday club for children on the other Sundays, and a community of parents which also meets together regularly.

They know that their team is not yet strong enough to launch all of this successfully so they are busy sharing their vision, with the idea of recruiting more team members. They have run some pilot versions of the proposed monthly event and have organised a dinner for the parents of all families known to be sympathetic to the church. They used this dinner to share vision, to answer questions and encourage people to share ideas.

At Oakington team building, research, and pilot events are all going on at the same time. This will eventually lead to the day when a firm proposal goes before the PCC for a new programme which will aim to do much more for the families of this village than is being attempted at present.

7. TARGETING

In 1990 we moved to Leicester, to a strong church which had been ministering successfully to people of all ages. I saw it as my long-term task to strengthen every area of this ministry. In the end I think I mainly succeeded, but at the beginning life was very difficult; I was preoccupied by conflicts and issues of trust, and the strong church which I had inherited had begun to stagnate. It took about four years before things settled down; then it was time to try to move the church forward again.

What I needed then was the notion of targeting. Targeting means choosing one group of people and in the short term being determined that, whatever else happens in the church, the ministry to that particular group is going to become strong. I wanted the church to welcome old people and middle-aged people; I wanted black and white, rich and poor; I wanted families and I wanted teenagers. All kinds of people must be included and feel that they mattered to the church and to me. I never abandoned this principle, but I knew that I could not get everything going at once, so I asked God to show me one group of people on whom I could focus.

The decision I made then was to place my main focus on the many young adults in my congregation who did not yet have children. Some were married, but most of them were single, and many were students. This became my target group and it remained my main target group for a number of years. Later I was able to switch the focus of my attention to other areas.

There were many reasons for this choice. Most important was the location of the church in the centre of the city; young adults are a very important group in any city. But this also was the group that was most on my heart, and it happened to be the group that I related to most easily.

I targeted these young adults through a lively evening service and a midweek group which we called Emerging Generation or 'EmGen'. I also raised some money from a wealthy sponsor to employ a young man whose job title was to be my personal assistant, but who was also given the task of recruiting his contemporaries, a task at which he was extremely good. Ed put the people he was recruiting into small groups, and these groups grew rapidly. We also employed interns to look after the students, and at a later stage took on a full time student minister, Vic, who stayed for about ten years; Vic also did a great job.

Targeting this one group became the foundation for developing and strengthening the whole church. Over the years, as these young adults grew older and had children they usually moved to the morning service and became involved in new activities targeted at whole families, at mothers and toddlers, at children, and at dads. But the emphasis on young adults without children has remained, and the evening service remains strong to this day. Important though the other ministries are, they are all still being fuelled by the success of the original ministry targeted at young adults. I think all city centre churches in university cities should go this way; but of course this kind of parish is unusual.

The Blue School in Wells

When I left Leicester and joined ReSource we moved to Wells in Somerset. In Wells I again wanted to work with younger people, but there are relatively few young adults living in Wells, so this time I decided to target secondary school children. This was because we had two fourteen year old daughters and all my easy contacts were with this age group. I began with prayer;  every day started with a prayer walk as the children were coming to school. Doors began to open. A vacancy was advertised for a parent governor and I was appointed. I started a chess club in the school and because I am a mathematician I began to support the maths staff, taking on some voluntary coaching. I discovered two other Christian families with children at the school and our families became friends. The school appointed a new chaplain and I became friends with her. Eventually we were able to set up a lunch time Christian Union. Numbers were quite small at first, but we concentrated on running high quality meetings, and bit by bit numbers grew as the original children brought their friends. Within two years we had twenty-five children meeting regularly at lunch time, and some of the original children had been formed into an effective team. I think this could be done in any secondary school.

But as before in Leicester it all depended on targeting. In Wells and in my work for ReSource I was involved with many things. But at that time I was determined that nothing would be as important to me as the teenagers at the school. I rarely missed a meeting of the lunchtime group, and I never missed team meetings. I committed myself to the relationships and made sure I got to know the parents of the children who came. If I had not made the decision to target this group, I think very little would have happened.

Mark's options

Every situation is different. Perhaps you will decide to target young adults, as I did in Leicester; perhaps you will choose to focus on teenagers, as I did in Wells. Whatever your situation you should prayerfully consider your options and decide.

> **Warning: Do not try to do too many things at once. Do one thing and do it well. Later, as your resources increase, you will be able to add a second target group and then a third and so on.**

Mark and his congregations have decided they want to welcome younger people in the church. In order to achieve this, they might choose to target any of the following groups:

- Whole families (fathers, mothers and children coming together)
- Young adults without children, some married, some single
- Fathers
- Primary school children
- Secondary school children
- Mothers with pre-school children
- Mothers with primary age children

I know of churches which are successfully targeting all of these groups, and churches which are targeting just one of them. The problem for Mark is that his church has been targeting none of them.

Of course eventually Mark will wish to have a ministry to all these groups, but to get going he will be wise to choose just one. So which of these groups will he and his team aim at first? This is a very important decision.

> Warning: It is important to consult widely about the vision to build a younger church. But do not allow the church council to determine the details; the decision on which target group to go for should be made by Mark and his team. There will be an important role for the church council when they are asked to endorse the specific proposal that Mark and the team will one day put before them.

Whole families – usually the best place to start

In Mark's position I would almost always choose to start with whole families. Most churches do not do this, and often experience serious negative consequences. Mark could for example do what many churches do: recruit a youth worker and begin by targeting teenagers. Perhaps this youth worker will be successful, as some are, and develop a ministry involving fifty teenagers. This would be a great achievement; but it would not help at all in developing a ministry to the other target groups. This is why stand-alone youth ministries tend to thrive for a while and then collapse. But if Mark begins with whole families and succeeds in recruiting fifty families, then in time a stable youth ministry will grow out of it as the original children grow older. This is precisely what happened during my time in Leicester. Our eventual thriving ministry to teenagers depended on the success of the ministry aimed at whole families which we had established ten years earlier. The order in which you target the various groups really matters.

Many churches in Mark's position choose to begin by targeting mothers and pre-school children through a mother and toddler club which meets on a weekday morning. Other churches decide to target mothers and primary age children with a weekday event which happens after school – an informal gathering with tea, or a Messy Church. Such clubs and events normally thrive, but when they meet during the working day far fewer men are involved. I question whether either a daytime mother and toddler or a weekday after-school event are the best way to start, simply because these events are not accessible to most fathers. If God is interested in whole families – fathers, mothers and children – then we should ensure that we are including and not excluding fathers in what we offer.

Taking a long term view, the evidence suggests it is normally best to start with an event which targets whole families, and therefore takes place at the weekend. My observation is that where this is being attempted it is usually successful. In an ideal world churches would have all three types of event: mothers and toddlers, an after-school event, and a weekend event for whole families. But if resources are limited then the weekend event is the one to go for first. As far as I can discern neither mother and toddler clubs or after-school clubs, however successful, seem to result in increased weekend attendance at church. On the other hand if a church can establish a successful weekend ministry which involves whole families, then it seems to be easy to open up the other activities later.

So Mark would be best to begin with a programme that focusses on whole families. This of course does not mean that people without children are excluded from the programme; indeed they are most welcome and will probably get a lot out of it. But when we say we are focussing on families we mean that we intend to judge the ministry mainly on how successful we are in recruiting and keeping families. This principle will govern everything that happens in the new programme.

> **Warning: If your aim is to reach families do not throw your energies and resources into midweek activities. First establish something at the weekend for whole families. Once this is thriving, consider adding some midweek activities as your resources permit.**

Of course, there sometimes are circumstances in which it would be better to go with a different target group than whole families; if that is the way that God leads then go that way. Indeed I began this chapter by giving examples of two situations in which I chose to target other groups, young adults in Leicester and teenagers in Wells. So later in this book, beginning with Chapter 22, I will try to show you how to go about it if you do decide on a different target group.

8. TEAM MEETINGS

As I explained in the last chapter, my greatest passion has been ministry to young adults. As with family ministry, to reach young adults and disciple them you need a core team. In the case of young adults, the main task of that team is to lead small groups, both enquiry groups and discipleship groups.

The thing I really looked forward to in Leicester was meeting with this team of small group leaders. Leading and training this team was a very important task. As the ministry grew in size so the team had to grow too; eventually we had more than 120 people coming to the team meeting. But there was a parallel meeting going on at the same time, a meeting of a different core team, the team who were leading the work among children. This meeting, led by the staff member responsible for children's work, was equally important.

Our team meetings were monthly. More than that puts too much pressure on busy people from whom we already expected a lot; less than that and you lose energy and vision, that sense of purpose in which the whole team must share. There were always those who struggled to get to the team meetings, but I was always fairly insistent about this, and each time we had a team meeting I repeated it at an alternative time for those who could not make it. That way practically everyone came.

> **Warning: Do not be afraid to insist that team members should come to team meetings. By coming to the meetings they will maintain their vision and improve their skills. Team meetings are not optional but essential.**

What do you do at a team meeting? Four things: fellowship, vision-casting, skills training, and prayer. The same structure can be used for the team meeting whatever the target group.

First make sure that the fellowship is good. For us this meant beginning with some food, and then putting people into groups to share news and pray for one another. At the end of the meeting we always had a time of worship so that people left feeling close to God.

Secondly, make sure you talk vision in the team meeting; I learned this a long time ago from the man who used to mentor me. Ed used to tell me "Whatever else you do, Roger, keep the vision clear!" At this stage Mark can best keep the team's vision clear by talking about children and his hopes for them – starting with his own children. I like to use Luke 2.52, which tells us that Jesus grew up physically, intellectually, socially, and spiritually. Today's children get the first three from their homes and schools, but the aim of our church is to have children who are growing up in all four dimensions. Mark should share his passion to raise children who are strong in their relationship with God, who love him and will serve him throughout their lives. He could explain how this works with his own children, and how he hopes to do the same for many children in the area. As time goes on the team will develop a vision for how this could be achieved, and there will be a lot to discuss.

> **Warning: When your team meets do not neglect sometimes to think five years ahead and imagine what the ministry might look like then. What will the children be like at that point? How many of them do you hope there will be? What activities will you be running for them? What do you hope to do to improve the quality of family life for these children?**

Then thirdly, use the team meetings to teach skills. You can only do a little at each meeting, but gradually the team will get better and better at what they are doing. With the team that I am leading at the moment we have just started to run all age services. We are gradually learning how to put together an all age service that keeps everyone engaged throughout and also succeeds in powerfully communicating God's word. It takes a lot of faith and skill to do this well, but the team is learning fast.

Finally, make sure that you do not neglect to pray together. The great thing about being involved with a team that has clear vision is that you all know exactly what you hope will happen, and this is a good place to be if you want to pray. Just make sure that you are praying with great confidence that God is going to bless the work to which he has called you.

9. THE NEW PROGRAMME

Let's assume that Mark and his team have decided on their target group – probably, but not necessarily, whole families. The next step is to devise a programme which will bring the people in this group into the orbit of the church. What activities should the team offer to the target group, and how should they get these going?

To answer that question let's think ahead five years. By then, if all goes well, the programme will have five parts. This would be true whatever the target group:

1. A regular worship event, tailor-made for the target group
2. A series of outreach events aimed at members of the target group who do not normally attend worship
3. A small group programme with groups both for believers and for not-yet believers
4. A social action programme
5. Ecumenical activities in partnership with other churches

First, as part of his programme, Mark must provide an opportunity for people to come together to worship God. Such worship events are likely to contain prayers, hymns, spiritual songs, Bible exploration and, where appropriate, Holy Communion. A good worship event is one in which God is very clearly present: where God speaks and acts and people respond in praise and worship. For this to happen, each event must be constructed round a particular passage of scripture or a biblical topic. In Chapter 17 I will give a detailed description of how a worship event targeted on whole families might work.

The second part of Mark's programme will be a series of outreach events which will draw in non-Christians as well as Christians. Each event will be based on a chosen theme which is then explored using talks, sketches, songs, games, craft activities and so on. A good outreach event tries to provide three things: a taste of community life, a place to belong, and a place to love and be loved. Outreach events should also provide take-home wisdom; the event is a learning experience, Christians and non-Christians discovering together ways to understand their lives and live them well.

And finally, while being very careful about the language used, a good outreach event will always explain the gospel and show its relevance to the chosen theme.

Outreach events do not have to be weekly. To be successful they have to reach very high standards, so it is much better to do four good ones a year than 52 mediocre ones. In Chapter 19 I will show how to plan an outreach event aimed at whole families.

Then thirdly, within five years Mark will also hope to have developed a small group structure to run alongside the worship and outreach events. Some of these small groups will be for believers, and will aim to provide fellowship and encourage discipleship. Other groups will be for enquirers and will aim to answer questions and encourage people to place their faith in Jesus. Small groups are an essential part of any ministry. Without small groups those who are not yet believers will not find faith, and those who are believers will not move on much in their discipleship. And without small groups relationships are likely to remain superficial.

If Mark decides to target families he will hope eventually to start groups for children, for mothers, dads, couples or, perhaps best of all, groups consisting of three or four families. Or there could be a group for parents which, amongst other things, meets to discuss how to be good parents.

A church exists, in part, to serve the community in which it is set, so whatever the target group an established ministry will eventually want to engage in constructive social action. If Mark does decide to target families then within five years he should aim to have started activities where families join together for the purpose of doing good to others, probably to other families. The first task is to discover what the key unmet needs are within your community; you can then devise a programme which will do something to meet those needs. Fun days, food banks and parenting courses are all possibilities.

Finally, within five years Mark will hope to have developed a partnership with other churches. Mark has Methodist, Baptist, Catholic and other churches within his parish. They are all part of the body of Christ in the area, and it will be good for the churches to love each other and sometimes work together. A shared programme emphasizes Christian unity, and may make it possible to achieve things that the churches would not be able to do by themselves.

Within the Anglican Church there are some very encouraging stories about churches with a thriving family work which then form a partnership with another church that has lost touch with children. Several families decide together to move from the thriving church and join the struggling one. I started with Donna and Alex. Donna began with a group of children who had just transferred from another church. In Leicester a group of families will soon transfer from Alex's church to join another Anglican parish. In both these examples the bishops have been involved and the change made to coincide with a change of vicar in the receiving church.

A summary of Mark and Rebecca's vision

Mark's churches are quite small, and no one would expect them to resemble a big city church. But based on the assumption that his initial target group will be families, this is a realistic vision for five years' time:

- A monthly all age worship service with twenty children coming regularly with their parents.

- A weekly Sunday Club on the other Sunday mornings for the same twenty children: after a short period in church the children are taught in small age-specific groups where they are learning to become disciples of Jesus.

- Because some of the original children have grown older there is an extra small group meeting which caters for children aged between ten and fourteen.

- An outreach event for families, happening five times a year, which attracts the twenty children plus twenty others, mostly friends of the church children.

- An annual holiday club which attracts a hundred children.

- A small discipleship group for mums meeting midweek with ten mums attending.

- A small discipleship group for couples meeting weekly with four couples attending.

- An enquiry group with ten adults attending.

- A social action programme aimed at helping the poor families living in the parish.

- Both the outreach events and the social action projects are run jointly with other churches in the town.

To achieve all of this in five years is quite feasible. If this is what happens then Mark and Rebecca will have built a foundation for future growth.

Making a start – the initial programme

This is what I hope Mark's programme will look like in five years' time; it's a picture for Mark to paint for his team, a vision of the future for them to believe in. But five years from now is not now; the question for now is how to get started. What kind of activity should Mark develop first? Should his team begin by starting a worship event, or some small groups, or a series of outreach events, or social action or what?

Normally the best way to start is with worship events. Almost anyone in Mark's position should be planning to start an all age worship event, one that is designed to attract and meet the needs of families but still welcomes people of any age.

In some places it works best to hold these all age events weekly. However a more popular alternative is to have an all age worship event just once a month and then offer a Sunday school on the other weeks when, after a short period of worship, the children leave their parents and are taught in small groups. The latter pattern is more attractive, but is only feasible in churches which have some side rooms. And it will only work well if Mark can find small group leaders who, like Donna and the team in Hampton Wick, really will disciple the children. In Chapter 18 I will discuss how this time in Sunday school can best be spent.

A third alternative, also quite popular, is to have Sunday school almost every week with only occasional all age services. This works well in churches with large numbers of children, but is not usually a good way of getting started in a parish like Mark's. Mark, to succeed, must recruit new families who have not been used to church before, and the easiest way is to provide an all age service where the families are not split up but can stay together.

Each of these patterns (all age services weekly, all age services monthly, Sunday school every week) enables families to come to church together and find something provided for every family member. Once Mark has a critical mass of families coming, experience shows that these families will start to bring others. And as the congregation grows the people who are joining will become the resources he will need not only to run the worship event but also to enable the outreach events, the small groups, and the social action.

Alternatives to starting with a worship event

But Mark doesn't have to start with a worship event, and there are undoubtedly alternatives to consider. For example, if most of the contacts Mark has initially are with sympathetic non-Christian families then it is probably best to start by launching a series of outreach events and to leave the development of worship events until later.

The well known Willow Creek ministry in Chicago began this way. The initial programme consisted of a series of outreach events (targeted at men) – what they called a 'church for the unchurched'. Once Willow Creek had established the outreach event they added small enquiry groups, and then later a regular worship event for the new Christians and for others who wished to join the church.

Mark could copy Willow Creek by starting with outreach events, but if he does then initially he will be providing no worship event for families to attend together. This would mean that families who want to attend worship must join in with whatever adult worship the church provides. Like Willow Creek, churches which begin with outreach usually hold their new events quite frequently, perhaps even weekly, so that there is always something available for children to come to. A compromise is possible; I know of churches which started their ministry to families by first holding a monthly all age worship service on a Sunday morning, and then adding a monthly outreach event on a different Sunday in the afternoon. Then as soon as they could they offered Sunday school on the other Sundays.

Warning: Before you start on anything consider all the options. Often churches put their resources behind the wrong plan simply because they have neglected to consider the alternatives.

In other places it will be simplest and best not to go for major events at all (neither worship or outreach events) but to start off with just one small group, not necessarily even one for children. One church leader I know found that at the beginning of her ministry her main opportunity was with a group of mums, none of whom were Christians, but all of whom were interested in going deeper. So she put all her other plans on hold and formed these mothers into an enquiry group. After they had all come to faith they began together on an activity for their children. This led on to outreach to the husbands and then to some experimental outreach events aimed at the whole village.

Another possibility is that many families in your area are troubled. In this case it may be best to begin not with a worship event, an outreach event, or a small group, but with social action. If you decide to go this way then your team should throw itself into some fairly high profile way of serving families and young people within the community. This should bring them into contact with many people, some of whom could later become the nucleus of a new worship event or a new outreach event, or could be brought into an enquiry group. The social action project, once begun, should not be stopped and should always remain as the heart of the ministry. I know of one church in north London that has begun this way. Things are going well; as a result of the social action project many children began to join in the Sunday services and from this the next stage has been to develop lively small groups for children. Now the children are starting to bring their parents to church with them.

Finally, in some situations it might be best to begin by working ecumenically right from the start. Suppose for example you have two churches from different denominations, each with small congregations; what neither church can do by themselves may be possible if they work together.

Churchill and Langford

Churchill and Langford are two villages close to Weston-super-Mare in Somerset. What the villages have in common is their Anglican priest and their Methodist minister. Kate and Julie are firm friends and prayer partners, and they see eye to eye. The Anglican Church in Langford has some children, but the other churches have none. Kate and Julie, working with a  joint Anglican-Methodist team, have decided to run all their children's activities jointly, with the exception of Sunday morning services. Mums and Tots and Youth Club happen in the Anglican Church. Messy Church, which they call Messy Gang, happens in the Methodist church, as does the club they run for 11-13 year olds.

10. A PROPOSAL FOR THE CHURCH COUNCIL

Once Mark and his team have decided on their target group and know what they hope the initial activities will be, then it is time to take a formal proposal to the church council and ask for their support.

Different churches govern themselves in different ways. Mark is an Anglican, which means that in making major changes he has to obtain the support of the PCC; this is especially true if any money is to be spent. But all denominations have an 'official' body which takes major decisions.

The official body, whatever it is, should have been consulted at the very early stage when the church was beginning to talk about the possibility of fresh vision. Mark will have asked them 'are we in favour of doing what we can to bring younger people into church?'. They will have said yes to this – this is what every church wants. And at that stage, without taking any votes, Mark will have asked the PCC for their ideas.

The official body will have been consulted again if Mark decided that he would like to recruit a new paid staff member. And it must be consulted again now that Mark and his team have a definite proposal to make about the way forward.

This proposal will need to cover the following:

- Definition of the target group to be reached by the new ministry, together with some idea of when it might be possible to move on to other target groups and what will be provided for them in the meantime.

- A list of the new activities which the team proposes to run – maybe initially just one new activity, for example a new all age service or a new social action project.

- The purpose of each proposed new activity: worship, outreach, small groups, social action, or ecumenical.

- The time and place of each proposed new activity and some idea of the date the team proposes to launch it.

- Who the core team are and what their roles will be; what help will be needed from others who are not part of the core team.

- A proposed budget showing how much the new ministry will cost.

- How and why the team believes the new activities are likely to draw in new people.

- The five year vision showing where all this is going.

In this proposal the budget is very important. Do not cut corners where finances are concerned. Aim for the highest possible standards in everything; if this means spending money, then so be it. Be very clear with the church council and ask for their support.

> **Warning: Do not try to bypass the church council; it is very important that fresh vision is owned by the whole church. Just make sure that you have done all that is needed to persuade them to own and support your proposals.**

> **Warning: Before you start on a new ministry be clear on how much money it is going to cost and where this money is going to come from.**

11. TIMES AND PLACES

Mark and his team may decide to start some small groups before they attempt anything else, but sooner or later they must decide to launch some bigger events – either worship events or outreach events. This leads to the question of where these events will take place and when.

Many years ago I remember launching a new event that would eventually prove to be the key to the growth of our church. This was not a worship event for families – we had one of those already – but a regular outreach event targeted at young adults. I had a capable team and also many founder members who I felt I could rely on, both to come to the event and also to invite non-Christian friends. We knew the style of the event which we wanted to run. All that remained was to decide where and when to hold it.

To research this we drew up a questionnaire and asked each of the founder members to survey their friends. They were to explain the style and purpose of the proposed event and then ask what would be the best place and time. The response to this survey was very clear. Nearly all these people, people who did not go to church themselves, suggested we hold the event in the church building – they said that would not put them off coming. They also advised us to hold it on Thursday evenings. So that is what we did.

Mark and his team must do something similar. It is no good holding the new worship or outreach event at a time when most families are doing something else, or in a place that will make them feel uncomfortable. So Mark must find a way of going to families and asking them what they think. If the advice that comes back is to hold a monthly all age service in the church on a Sunday morning, this would be very convenient for Mark because that is what would cause the least disruption to his current programme. But if the advice is different, Mark must be ready to make changes. In some places many families are involved in sports activities on a Sunday morning; if that is what Mark finds and he is serious about reaching families then he will need to switch to another time.

> Warning: Do not choose the time and the place for a new worship service on the basis of either church tradition or church politics. Do not choose it to suit your own convenience either. Base your decision on what you are learning about the target group and their preferences.

The right place

The right place to hold the new events may well be the church building, but it may not. For example one church where I am working at the moment still has its old pews, and we think this would be a big turn-off for new people. And the all age service which we have in mind will work much better if there is more freedom of movement. So for the time being we have decided to use the hall at the church school. The families we are hoping to attract are very comfortable with the school, but unfamiliar with the church.

The really important thing is to have enough space but not too much. Suppose for example that you have six team members and five families – about twenty-five people in all. The event will work really well in a small space, but not in a large church. So start off in a space which fits the size of the group and move later when the numbers have increased.

> Warning: Avoid holding meetings for a few in a large church building. Consider holding the new event in someone's home or in a suitable community building. If it is important to you to use the church building, use a side chapel or a side room or perhaps the chancel area.

The right time

There are many options for the timing of the new events. There is clear evidence that all of these have worked well in one place or another.

Option 1 – breakfast

The first possibility is to centre the new series of events on breakfast, either on Saturday or Sunday – probably breakfast at 8.30 and then an event which runs from 9 to 9.45. This approach was adopted very successfully by Christine Froude when she was vicar of Shirehampton in the Diocese of Bristol. Christine had no one to start with, but eventually large numbers came.

It seems that early morning is a good time for families – when you have small children you do not get a lie-in just because it is the weekend! By providing a good breakfast the events become attractive to dads, and if older children need to go off to sports later in the morning they will still be able to do so.

Option 2 – a second morning service

Some churches change their Sunday pattern to make room for two morning services. For example some begin with a traditional service at 9.30 and follow this with the new family event at 11.

I am in touch with one church which adopted this pattern and then, some years later, switched back to just having one service. By this stage the families were sufficiently integrated and numerous to have a big say in the design of the joint service, and traditionally-minded members were much more prepared to compromise than they would have been if a joint service had been attempted right from the start. At the beginning traditionalists had been very willing to welcome families with open arms – but only to a service which in practice was little changed.

St John's, Penistone

David Hopkin at Penistone has opted to put his service for families before the traditional service, which seems to be the better way round, though David feels in retrospect that to hold the second service only one hour after the first seems a bit cramped.

David went to Penistone in 2005 and found a church that had no children at all. He immediately launched a Sunday school in a community centre, and the children who came were brought into church to join in with communion. This was a compromise that did not work too well, and in 2008 David replaced the Sunday school by a family service starting at 9.45am. The initial families came through contacts that David had made in the community, but subsequent growth has come mainly through baptism contacts. As I have seen elsewhere, it is the family service that persuades the baptism parents to keep coming, and to date more than 50% of them remain in the church. There are twenty families coming now and there seems every reason to think that David is meeting a need and that the growth will continue.

Two other features of David's work seemed important to me. David keeps a database of his contacts, making communication and publicity very easy. Even more important, he has recruited a leader for the family service who, though unpaid, is able to be there every week and is very good at communicating from the front. This means that having a family service does not put David under pressure, even though he has five churches to cover.

Option 3 – an alternative morning service

A third possibility is to introduce the new event at the same time as the current morning service but in a different building.

Milford-on-Sea

This approach has worked very well at Milford-on-Sea. Milford had developed a large and spiritually strong congregation, but its services were quite traditional and were not popular with families. The decision was made to cater for families by holding a parallel service in the church hall, and a new family worker was recruited and given responsibility for the new service.

So at Milford families came to the church hall services and everyone else could choose – most opted to stay where they were. Periodically the two services were merged. Numbers at the traditional service remained the same but numbers at the new service grew rapidly. It helped that the band which led the music at the new service was of a very high standard. It was observable that many dads were coming to the new service and enjoying the informality which gave them the opportunity to move around and interact with their friends. Very few young men enjoy services in which there is no movement and no opportunity to say anything; this is an increasing problem with traditional services.

> **Warning: When choosing the time and place for the new event pay the greatest attention to how the young men, the children's dads, will experience it. Making dads feel comfortable is extremely important.**

Option 4 – a monthly all age service

Probably the most common pattern of all is to introduce an all age service which happens monthly and replaces the usual morning service on that Sunday. As the next step a Sunday school is provided on the other weeks so that there is something for children every week.

If you go for this option, avoid the pattern which I have often seen. An elderly congregation under pressure from a new vicar agrees to give up their normal Sung Eucharist once a month and to replace it with all age worship led by guitars. What happens is that the same people turn up plus just one or two families, and the service is dreary, with no one enjoying it very much.

Mark himself has inherited just such a situation – when he arrived there was already a monthly all age service, but almost no children came to it. Mark will probably decide to keep this pattern, but will relaunch the service once he has recruited some new families.

Holywell

An interesting example comes from Holywell in North Wales. In 2009 John Lomas, the vicar, found himself ministering on Sundays to a congregation of grandmothers. If any children came, which they did occasionally, they were provided with toys, tables, and crayons to play with at the back of the church, while the grandmothers and John enjoyed a traditional Anglican service.

Most people who are brought up in Holywell remain in the town as adults, so most of these grandmothers are very involved in the lives of their grandchildren – who often live just round the corner. John hit on the idea of persuading the grandmothers to start bringing their grandchildren to church.

He began by talking to the congregation about sacrifice, asking them to give up one service a month for the sake of their grandchildren. So it was that the monthly children's service was launched. A lot of children came on that first Sunday. The toys, tables and crayons were moved to the front of the church. John found a good musician who played songs which the children were used to singing at school.

Each service was themed, was planned and led by a team, and lasted for just forty minutes. This was followed by refreshments, and John made sure he was able to stick around. Very soon the mothers of the children started to come as well, and then a bit later some of the fathers. Sunday school was arranged for the other Sundays, and now runs in parallel to the traditional service. The age profile had been completely reversed and the congregation was doubled. What John did in Holywell would probably work in any working class community.

St Andrew's, Holt

Andrew Evans is the vicar of St Andrew's in Holt, a village near Trowbridge. Six years ago when Andrew arrived there was no children's work, but Andrew is good with children and became popular in the primary schools. This led on to the establishment of a lively all age service which happens once a month in church. This service lasts for about fifty minutes; everyone is  together throughout the time. There is always a talk, some songs (often action songs) prayers and a Bible reading; there is also fun and movement and laughter. Puppets are used and sketches performed; those who want to can dance. On the other weeks of the month a short period of all age worship is followed by everyone meeting in their own age group.

Option 5 – a modified morning service

Other churches have not changed their service times at all, but instead have tried to modify the usual morning service so as to make it more attractive to families. The structure of the service, the music choices, and the style and content of the teaching are made more accessible to families. Once the changes have been agreed it is best to launch the new service with a blaze of publicity and advertising so that a lot of families come on that first week. It is essential that right from the start everyone realises that a radical change has taken place.

Holy Trinity, Cirencester

Howard Gilbert became leader of Holy Trinity Cirencester in 2009. When Howard arrived, Holy Trinity had a pattern of Eucharistic services with Sunday school and crèche on three Sundays, and an all age service on the fourth Sunday.

There were then an average of ten children each week, some in the crèche, some in the Sunday school. Howard's question was 'Do ten children constitute a critical mass, or is ten too few? Could the situation be turned round without doing something really radical?'

Howard decided that ten was just enough but that the problem needed his immediate attention. So he talked to everybody about it, and discovered that the families did not really feel welcome, and the older people were not very happy about them being there. What Howard did was to bring the two sides together and thrash it out. How could they modify the service so that families were properly integrated with the older congregation? Howard found that both sides listened, and the result has been a whole series of minor changes and great improvements in the relationships. Now, four years later, the services are enjoyed by all and the number of children has gradually increased so that ten children have become twenty-five.

I doubt very much if this could have been achieved apart from the fact that both the crèche leader and the Sunday school leader are outstanding individuals who have embraced Howard's vision and tried their best to make it work. Fiona in particular has worked hard to create a sub-community of parents who know each other well, so that when new families arrive they have been easily assimilated.

The Itchen Valley

A similar story comes from Andrew Micklefield, who became vicar of a rural parish near Winchester in 2010. Like Howard in Cirencester, Andrew realised that the number of children in his church community was dangerously low. Most of the children came to just one service a month, the family service. Andrew decided that something of good quality must be  provided every week, and his wife Fiona set about recruiting a team. Fiona also spoke to the families themselves to find out what they really wanted, and in response to this a weekly Sunday school named 'The Ark' opened in the local village hall.

From the start Fiona aimed for high standards. The children get ten minutes all together, and are then taught in four separate age groups, including a crèche; finally they join the church service for communion.

Once Andrew knew that the children who came would enjoy being there, he set out to recruit more. When a new family moved into the parish they would get a visit from Andrew and a welcome pack from the church. Baptisms were taken seriously and followed up by an invitation to join a weekly mother and toddler club. Andrew then offered a course on parenting which proved extremely popular.

Three years later the average number of children in church each week is fifteen, and the church feels as if it is already an all age congregation. Small beginnings, but because good foundations have been laid I would expect to see steady growth in the years ahead.

Option 6 – Sunday tea time

A worship event does not necessarily have to take place in church, and it does not have to be on a Sunday morning. Neither do outreach events. So some churches have decided to leave Sunday morning as it is and start a new event for families at Sunday tea time; the event always includes eating tea together. There is no doubt that in most places more families are available at tea time on Sunday than at any other time during the week.

St James, Trowbridge

Rob Thomas became the vicar of St James, Trowbridge in 2010. After being in post for about five months, Rob and his wife Marilyn launched TT, a completely new service for families which takes place on Sunday afternoons at 4.30pm. The service is in church and lasts for twenty-five minutes; afterwards everyone stays for tea. The structure of the service is quite  simple: some familiar bits of liturgy, some songs, some prayers. The atmosphere is informal and everyone sits in a circle in the huge chancel area. During the service the children are brought together for a Bible story, while Rob speaks for a few minutes to the parents.

To get this going Rob and Marilyn began with the existing midweek mother and toddler club. They started attending the club, got to know the people, and then eventually asked if anyone would be interested in a new monthly tea time service. Baptism contacts were also invited. Many people were positive and the first time that TT happened forty-nine people came (10 team, 16 parents, 23 children). Numbers grew and the service now happens twice a month. Rob is about to recruit a family worker who will aim to develop a personal ministry to the people who are coming to this service, something which Rob himself does not have time for. The first task for this new worker will be to recruit a core team to work alongside her.

Option 7 – a weekday

The final option is to have the new event on a different day of the week to Sunday. An after-school event starting at 3.30pm is a common pattern, though how working parents are supposed to be there beats me. Of course you could try Saturday!

3.30pm on a weekday works well if the chosen target group is not whole families but mothers with school age children. To get the dads there you could try starting at 6pm and beginning with a meal – but I don't know of any church that has tried this.

12. IDENTIFYING FOUNDER MEMBERS FOR THE NEW PROGRAMME

I lose count of the number of times I have attended what is billed as an all age service only to find that there are sixty or seventy adults present but very few children. Services like this never work; they only work once you have a critical mass of families.

Ideally Mark will need to start with ten families, though perhaps five would be enough. Once Mark has ten families they will soon become friends, and once this friendship circle is established they will all enjoy coming to the event and will start to bring other families. Any new family trying the event out will be easily absorbed. But if the event has only two or three families to start with it is likely to limp along and never really take off.

So new events, be they worship events or outreach events, should not be launched until you are confident that a critical mass of families will be present in the very first week. This means that the next task for Mark and his team is to recruit these founder members. In some places this may take quite a long time; in others it will be quite easy.

> **Warning: Do not set up a new event and advertise hoping that people will come. Instead first find your founder members and get their commitment to the event.**

Most churches have a few families who attend church sometimes and so are well known to the church leaders. These families are prime candidates to be founder members for the new event. The team should approach these people, share the vision for a new family programme, ask their advice, and try to recruit them.

Other churches already have midweek events for children; some have a successful mother and toddler club, others have a midweek Messy Church, some already run children's clubs. All these activities are potential recruiting grounds for founder members. The team should get to know the people, ask their advice, and explain what the new event could do for their families.

If none of this works Mark and his team must redouble their efforts to make friends. They can go into schools, mingle at the school gate, hold parties for children, run one-off events for families like a Christingle service, or a service which explains Easter, or a light party at Halloween, or a family treasure hunt in the summer. They could run a holiday club, raise funds for the school, organise a fete, offer hospitality.

So share your vision, and pray. Pray to be led to families who are open. You may find founder members very quickly, but if not don't give up but keep on praying and working at it. When you have five to ten families then it is time to launch the new programme.

Beyond this, especially for Anglicans, there are two tried and tested methods which will usually produce lots of founder members. The first way is to look amongst baptism contacts. The second is to form a partnership with the local primary schools, especially if they are church schools.

13. BAPTISMS

During my researches for this book I have discovered to my surprise that requests for infant baptism seem to be on the increase. It seems that once they have children many couples who lost contact with the church years earlier begin to think seriously about the way they want to bring those children up; and so they ask for baptism.

Back in Corby in the 1980s I did my quota of infant baptisms, as everyone does. But looking back on it I don't think I got it quite right. My all-consuming aim then was to make converts amongst adults, and I saw every funeral, wedding, or baptism not only as a pastoral responsibility but also as an opportunity for evangelism. We did see a lot of adult converts in Corby, but relatively few of them came through what we Anglicans call the 'occasional offices'.

Recently, though, I have been meeting some clergy who are succeeding in recruiting up to 50% of their baptism contacts into long term membership of the church. I have asked myself how they do this. The answer seems to be that they have a different aim to the one I had in Corby. My aim was to make more adult converts; but the successful clergy today are those who offer not commitment but belonging. Their aim is simply to recruit families to join the church community. Commitment can come later.

Once you understand this you see that what matters most is not the baptism preparation classes but the attractiveness of the community which you are encouraging the new family to join, and the way that you go about introducing the new family to that community.

Mark should begin by using the church notice board and website to make it obvious how people can contact him if they want their children baptised. If Mark has established a good reputation in the community, people will come. When they do, he should offer a baptism course at which parents will be helped to understand the meaning of Christian baptism, the implications of the promises which they will make, and the meaning of the promises which the church will make in committing itself to the spiritual welfare of their children. The baptism classes begin the process of communicating the gospel to the new family.

But it is what happens after the baptism classes that really matters. What comes next is the baptism service, and this is where things can start to go wrong. The church gathers for its usual Sunday morning service. The baptism party arrives – usually a band of mainly young people dressed as if for a wedding. The church service is exactly what they expected: friendly and welcoming, but essentially weird. They like the vicar, who is going out of his or her way to help them; but the church members, being nearly all a generation older than the people in the baptism party, completely fail to connect. So do the hymns, the prayers, the organ, the liturgy and almost everything else about the service. One thing you can be sure of is that the baptism party will not be in church next week.

What can be done about this? Well – imagine Mark's church as I hope it will be in five years' time. By then there is an event to which lots of families, including babies, come every week. At his first meeting with the new couple Mark will explain that the church has many people like them who are trying to bring their children up to live in relationship with God and to embrace a Christian lifestyle. When you have a child baptised you are making a decision to join this community, so he would like the new couple to try the community out. When they are ready the baptism can take place at one of the community events. Meanwhile Mark would like them to attend baptism classes, and he will invite one of the other couples from the community to come as well. When the new couple come to the event they find something which is very unlike a traditional church service; it feels as if the service is tailor-made for people like them. They even understand the language that is being used!

Well of course Mark is not there yet. He does not have the community in place. But he does have a vision for it, so he can share his vision with every new baptism family, he can introduce them to the team, and he can try to extract a promise that when the time comes this family will consider becoming founder members for the new service. I am suggesting that Mark should be vulnerable, open about his hopes and fears, taking the new couple into his confidence.

Warning: Do not conduct a baptism service in the context of a normal church service if you fear that the service may feel weird to the baptism party. It has to seem to the baptism party that this is a community where they could easily fit in.

Christ Church, New Malden

Under its leader Stephen Kuhrt this church has developed a model for family worship which works well. Their event lasts from 9.30am until 10.20am. The middle section, which lasts for thirty minutes, offers a sermon to the adults while their children enjoy age-appropriate activities. The parents can opt for the sermon or join in with their children. Twelve minutes  at the beginning are used for all age worship, with colouring books provided for the youngest children, and eight minutes at the end allows children to report back on what they have been doing.

This family worship event has been deliberately made very attractive to couples bringing a new baby, one idea being to make a DVD of the baptism service and to present this to the family. And great emphasis is laid not just on the responsibility of the parents to keep their vows, but also on the responsibility of the church to commit itself wholeheartedly to the new family. This has led to a considerable growth in numbers.

I have not been to the services at Christ Church, so I have to use my imagination. What I imagine is a service with lots of children from very small babies to much older ones. Then I imagine a new family trying out the service a few weeks before the baptism. The new couple readily find acceptance and friendship and continue coming until the baptism is done. Isn't it likely that this family will keep on coming and, finding many new friends, be quickly absorbed into the church community?

St Michael and All Angels, Hilperton

Hilperton (the largest of four village churches which make up a benefice near Trowbridge) has a thriving ministry to families, led by the vicar Stephen Ball, which has emerged from the many requests he gets for baptisms (200 in four years), mostly from families with professional backgrounds. Four years ago there was nothing for families in Hilperton. Now there are fifty very regular attenders.

When parents come to seek baptism for their child, Stephen always begins by asking what they think baptism is for. He then explains that baptism is the beginning of the child's journey of faith, implying that if the journey is to begin it needs to be on the understanding that it will continue. Stephen explains that in the service the parents promise to bring the child up within the life of the church, but probably even more important is the church's promise to continue to be a resource to the parents. He goes on to ask the parents about their own spiritual journey – how did it begin, and how is it continuing? And do the parents too need some help? He finds it helpful to quote the African proverb that it takes a whole village to raise a child, and then say that the church would like to do its best to be that village.

The parents are then invited to join in with the programme, which consists of a twice monthly family service on a Sunday morning and a monthly service on Wednesdays. Some come on Sundays, some on Wednesdays, and some come to both. The content and timing of this programme was designed at a meeting between Stephen and the parents, and is under constant review by them all. The baptisms take place at these services.

Cherhill, Wiltshire

Philip Bromiley is the vicar of Cherhill and five other rural parishes. Philip's own children are the only children attending Sunday church. But there have been a lot of baptisms over the last five years, and Philip decided to run a one-off event to which he

could invite these baptism families. This was not a worship but an outreach event. The theme was 'superheroes' and every child was asked to come in fancy dress representing the superhero of their choice. At the event Jesus was revealed as the super-superhero. Rather to Philip's surprise the church was packed, and the same thing happened when Philip ran a second event.

This time Philip asked those who were interested in a regular event to leave their email addresses. Many did, and the next stage will be to call a meeting (cheese & wine at the vicarage) to see what may be possible. It may be that Philip will have the founder members he needs for a new event with remarkably little effort. It strikes me that this approach would work almost anywhere.

> **Warning: Keep a list of the children who have been baptised**
> **in your church and from time to time put something on for them.**
> **These families will remain well disposed towards the church.**
> **reason they never come is due, at least in part, to the fact that the**
> **church is not yet providing anything which they can connect with.**

14. CHURCH SCHOOLS

Some incumbents will find that they have one or more church schools within their patch. If you have such schools, then the task of developing family work will be much easier. In those where the head is a committed Christian it should be very easy indeed to get things going. A Christian head in a church school is likely to be very interested in developing a shared vision for both school and church.

I would recommend that new incumbents with church schools make immediate contact with the headteacher and the chair of governors, and when the opportunity arises also with the staff, the school council, and any parent groups. It is also helpful to go and see the diocesan director of education and the diocesan schools improvement advisor. With all these people, discuss ways in which the church can best support the school.

> **Warning: If your parish has a church school do not miss the opportunity this provides, especially in those places where the headteacher is a committed Christian.**

All church schools are subject to statutory inspection through the SIAMS (Statutory Inspection of Anglican and Methodist Schools) process which judges a school according to its Christian character. The criteria are clearly laid down; a school is judged as outstanding only if the children are being taught the essence of the Christian faith on a daily basis through everything that happens in the school.

I visited one such school in the village of Kingsland, Herefordshire. What happens in this school beats anything that any church could hope to do. If I were the local vicar I would be telling myself that the school is already doing my job for me, and I would want my church community to support the school in any way we could.

In any school some pupils and some teachers will not be Christians, and making them feel uncomfortable cannot be a good policy for the school. Neither must the school engage explicitly in evangelism. But any church school which tries to be outstanding by the SIAMS criteria is bound to have a significant impact on the faith choices being made by every person involved in the school, adult or child. There are four distinct ways in which a church school may make its impact:

- A church school seeks explicitly to teach Christian values and live by them every day. By joining a church school as pupil or teacher you accept that Christian values will dominate, and you open yourself to learning everything you can about the Christian way of conducting relationships, or handling disappointment, or working hard, or whatever comes up in school life.

- A church school seeks to teach pupils how to have a relationship with God, for example through prayer and worship experiences. This is to be normal school life. Care must be taken about the language used, and opt-outs made available for pupils who do not wish to participate in Christian worship. But in schools like Kingsland children are encountering God on a daily basis just as surely as they encounter trees or birds or football or mathematics.

- A church school will explain Christian doctrine, for example about God, about Jesus, about the Holy Spirit. The doctrine explains why the values we live by are important, and why we go about prayer, Bible study and worship in the way that we do. In practice any child who spends several years in one of these schools will emerge with a basic understanding of the Christian faith. At the same time, believing in Christian doctrine has to be presented as a choice, and not believing has to be seen in the school as a valid choice.

- Finally, a church school will advocate Christian commitment, though it must do this implicitly (for example through the very impressive lifestyle of the Christian staff that I met at Kingsland). The explicit urging of Christian commitment must be left to the church; but there is no reason why this cannot be done out of school hours but still on school premises.

Warning: A church leader with a church school in the parish has an opportunity and a responsibility. Don't miss these through a failure to understand what church schools are all about. Church leadership brings many pressures but this is one to accept wholeheartedly.

Many incumbents find themselves linked to a church school where the headteacher is committed to the SIAMS criteria. If so the policy of the church team should be to commit to the school in any way that the headteacher finds helpful. For example:

- By contributing to assemblies
- By contributing to RE teaching in the school
- By providing 'Open the Book' (a programme of themed and dramatised Bible stories)
- By encouraging the school to use the church for festivals (Easter, Christmas, Pentecost, Mothering Sunday etc)
- By allowing the church school to use the church for special events (drama productions, beginning and end of term services etc)
- By ensuring that if children come to services at the church the songs they sing will be the same as the ones they sing at school
- By contributing to staff training days (how to teach Christian values, how to help children pray and worship, how to explain Christian doctrine, the issue of how and whether to talk about Christian commitment)
- If the school has a logo, to include the logo in church publicity, websites etc
- Some schools, like Kingsland, have groups of like-minded people (parents, staff, governors) who work together to discern how the school's character can best be expressed and developed. If these groups exist the church team should be wholeheartedly involved.
- By working together on joint projects involving music or drama, for example ones linked to the church year
- By using particular skills to enhance school life (for example helping with sports, drama, music, art, chess)
- Through members of the parish serving on the Governing Body of the school as Foundation or parent governors, thus bringing professional expertise, experience and partnership into the life of the school.

From the point of view of the church team this should all be extremely rewarding. If the church does nothing else then undoubtedly massive numbers of seeds will have been sown, in the lives of the children and in those of their families. But this by itself is not enough: the church team will also want to have a hand in reaping as well as sowing – not in twenty years' time but here and now.

This will mean that the church team will want to offer additional activities, not instead of supporting the school but as well as. Here are some possibilities, in the order in which they are normally best established:

- The introduction of a regular all age worship service, held in church or on school premises depending on local circumstances. The school could be asked to provide a choir or a drama group for this service. The close involvement of the team with the school would be likely to produce large numbers of founder members for this worship event.

- The provision of an after school club, probably weekly, which as well as being great fun also teaches Christian values, worship, doctrine and commitment.

- The provision of a confirmation class for year 6 pupils.

- The introduction of a series of outreach events, maybe a Messy Church activity, possibly at the end of the school day, but more likely on Saturday or Sunday afternoon.

This is all going to work much better if the headteacher is wholeheartedly behind it. The head cannot be expected to lead these extra sessions and will only be able to attend occasionally, but he or she should have a controlling voice regarding where and when they happen, and what is taught. It should be a cardinal principle for the team that they will listen very carefully to any reservations the head may have.

> **Warning: If at all possible become good friends with the headteacher at your church school. The head has a tough job and needs your constant support and encouragement. So don't fail to put time into this.**

Trull, Somerset

Ross Hathway became the vicar of Trull, a village near Taunton, in 1992. When he arrived there were hardly any children involved in church, but the parish had a church school.

Ross began by networking widely within the village. He wanted to become a well known and respected figure, and achieved this very quickly. He saw his reputation in the village, not just his reputation in the church community, as of vital importance.

Ross made particular friends with the headteacher, whom he was eventually able to lead to faith in Jesus. He worked hard at supporting her in school assemblies and RE teaching.

The next stage was to establish a Friday evening club for children on the church premises. The school helped in advertising the club and because the whole village thought well of Ross, it was well attended right from the start. There was a mix of games, fun, food, worship, and Christian teaching.

Then Ross launched a monthly family service on Sunday morning, moving the usual Eucharistic service to an earlier slot. The new family service was advertised through the school and through the club. The headteacher came, and groups from the school played a part in music and drama. The service featured the use of puppets, which Ross's wife Alison had already used skilfully both in the school assemblies and in the Friday night club.

From that beginning the work amongst families has grown and grown. The exodus of Christian families to church in nearby Taunton has stopped and twenty years later the work is still thriving, even though Ross and Alison have moved on.

15. PRIMARY SCHOOLS WHICH ARE NOT CHURCH SCHOOLS

In Mark's parish the primary schools are not church schools; Mark is yet to discover what the attitude of these schools will be. In some non-church schools the involvement of the church is just as welcome as it would be in a church school; other headteachers are more cautious. Even so the school is where the families that Mark wants to reach are to be found, and so he must make every effort. My own approach has been to write to the headteacher introducing myself, asking for an appointment, and promising to follow up my letter with a phone call.

> **Warning: Do not fail to make contact with the headteachers of the primary schools in your patch. You could be missing out on what could be a golden opportunity to form a partnership which will be fruitful for both school and church.**

All primary schools have to follow an Agreed Syllabus for religious education, and all primary schools are required to provide assemblies of a broadly Christian character. Mark could begin by offering to assist the school with both of these.

Mark should also express willingness to help the school in any other way he can. My own approach has been to offer to run a chess club in the school, or to become a governor; I have found that both of these are very welcome. If roles like this are not for Mark himself then they could be for the team leader or team members.

Headteachers are normally admirable people who share many of Mark's values even if they do not share his beliefs. They are also vulnerable people who need friendship and encouragement. Whatever the head's views Mark should make himself available, hoping to become a trusted friend and source of support. In any school, once Mark and the church team are trusted, they will find many opportunities for pastoral ministry, not least among the teaching staff who often find themselves feeling tired and discouraged.

All primary schools are charged with making links between the school and the community. So Mark should explain his vision for a regular worship event or regular outreach event, consult the head on style, content and timing, and invite the school to participate. It may also be helpful to hold these events on school premises.

> Warning: If you are looking for founder members for your new programme, don't miss the opportunity to ask the local primary schools to provide a choir or a drama group. If the school says yes this will bring new families into the church very easily.

16. LAUNCHING THE NEW PROGRAMME

Decisions have been made. You have decided on your initial programme. You know when things are going to happen and where. You have recruited some founder members who are positive about joining in from the start. All that remains is to decide on a launch day for the new programme and then to advertise thoroughly.

By this time you should have developed many contacts with families; the team should design an attractive invitation, similar to one you would use for a birthday party, and send it out to all those contacts, delivered by hand wherever possible. If you have contact with local schools ask if you can do a presentation at the assemblies and then send the children home with invitation cards.

It may help to have a trial run for a few weeks before you have the big launch. Keep the trial run for the founder families, and then launch the event with a splash of publicity. The event can of course be relaunched again and again.

> **Warning: The first time that an event is held is very significant, so do not go ahead without thorough advertising.**

Oakhill, Somerset

This story is about the Methodist church in Oakhill, a small village in Somerset. At one time this church had a typical Methodist congregation consisting of a small number of faithful older people. Then Gary and Ann Ralls moved into the village with their two small children.

The older folk at the church gave them a wonderful welcome; Gary and Ann knew that they wanted to stay and bring their family up in this church. But they also realised that to make this work they would have to recruit more families.

They began with the local school, an Anglican church school, where they were welcomed and began to do regular assemblies. Gary is a great story-teller and the children loved those assemblies. But how to get the children to make the short journey from the school to the Methodist church?

Gary and Ann consulted the church leaders and decided on a launch date. Everyone prayed hard. Invitations to the launch day were sent home through each child in the school. The big day came and, to everyone's surprise, on that Sunday morning fifty children arrived at church with their parents. Gary and Ann made sure the children had a good time and the church people did their best to give the parents a welcome. Some families only came once, but in the end the church succeeded in keeping twenty-five of the children. So Gary and Ann's children had some new friends. This eventually turned into the most effective youth work in that part of Somerset.

17. ALL AGE SERVICES

All age services are ones in which children and adults stay together throughout. For most of my time as a church leader I avoided them if I possibly could. The problem for me was the sermon; I noticed that very few people seemed to have the skill to successfully address all ages at the same time – and I didn't think I was one of them!

So mostly I preferred the Sunday school system where quite early on in the service the children go off to another room or rooms and are taught separately. Sometimes the children return near the end of the service so that they can join in with communion.

Later I discovered that it is quite easy to do an all age service provided you follow some simple rules – rules which also apply to the all age parts of other services. Having looked at many different models, I have come to the conclusion that in a small church like Mark's it is probably best to aim for a mixture: perhaps once a month an all age service, and something more like a traditional Sunday school on the other weeks, when a sermon can be offered for adults while the children are out. Here are some simple rules for all age services:

- Always divide the service into sections, with each section lasting only a very few minutes. This is necessary to make concentration possible for all age groups. So no long talks or sermons – this is the first and most important principle. There are more ways to teach people than by talking continuously for twenty minutes.

- Make sure that some sections of the service are very quiet and others are quite rowdy with plenty of noise and movement.

- Use more than one voice to lead the service; probably several, but at least two. A good all age service is led by a team.

- Seat the congregation in groups and include two or three sections of group work. Groups should be four or five people with both adults and children in each group. This can be made to work even if you have pews.

- Make sure that each section is comprehensible to all but the smallest children. The ideas may be profound but the language must be child friendly. Adults will not mind this at all.

- Do not differentiate between adults and children; treat them all the same. Do not allow the adults to become spectators.

- Use visuals – make sure that there is plenty to look at.

- Have plenty of movement – do not leave people sitting still for long periods.

- Choose music which everyone knows and loves – even the smallest children and the crustiest of adults. This probably means having a small repertoire to begin with, but you can slowly build it up.

If you follow these rules there is no need for the service to be short – an hour is a good length. Keep each section short, but if all the sections are biblically based and full of life and energy then the whole service will be infused with God's presence, and sixty minutes will pass very quickly. Someone wisely said that sermonettes make Christianettes – the same is true of very short all age services.

Preparing for an all age service

Like any other church service, an all age service is about engaging with the word of God. So I try to approach my preparation with the conviction that God is going to speak, and that as a result lives will change. Unless you share this conviction, you and your team will not lead the service well, no matter how skilled you are at keeping things lively and interesting. There is no need for all age services to be superficial – they can be used to feed an entire congregation, adults and children alike.

Preparation for an all age service should always begin with some Bible study, either a Bible passage or a biblical theme. When I lead an all age service I begin by selecting the biblical material carefully and then sending it to the team. The team are asked to study the material prayerfully, paying particular attention to two things:

1. What does the biblical material teach – about God, Jesus, the Holy Spirit, the world, ourselves?

2. What is the appropriate way for those who come to the service to respond? God is always looking for two kinds of response: first a response of obedience where, having heard the Lord's command, we commit ourselves to live in a way that pleases him; and secondly a response of trust where, having understood what God is promising to do in our lives, we trust him to do it. So the question is 'what are the obedience responses to the Bible passage, and what are the trust responses?'

   Warning: Do not build an all age service round a sketch, or a good story, or anything other than a Bible passage or a biblical theme. If the clever ideas you have do not fit, leave them to be used on another occasion. What matters is that the message of the Bible should do its powerful work in the lives of the congregation.

In one church where I am working, the team meets about three weeks before each event. They come prepared, having studied the Bible passages for themselves, and ready to share ideas for how the service might go. There are nine on the team, so if we have one or two good ideas each we have more than enough material. Everything we teach is rooted in the chosen Bible passages, but team members are also encouraged to research the internet and consult books (see the book list at the end).

To illustrate what I mean here is the outline of a recent all age service held in the school hall. The ideas for this outline came from all nine team members. There were twenty children present and fifty-seven adults. The whole service lasted sixty minutes. The subject was 'The Creation' and the biblical passages which we studied in preparation were: Romans 1.19-20; Psalm 14.1-2; Genesis 1.26-27; Psalm 8.3-6; Psalm 139.13-14; Psalm 23.6. The service was put together after the team meeting, using the team's ideas and giving each of them a role.

All age service Oakington September 2014

- Philip is a member of the all age service team and the leader of the music group. He began the service with a hymn (Praise to the Lord, the almighty, the King of creation) and said a prayer inviting the Lord into the service.

- Jacob gave out party poppers and asked people to set them all off at once. What is the connection between the opening song and the noise? The answer of course was the Big Bang, the phrase science uses for God's creation. Jacob told everybody that this would be the subject today.

- Philip led in a song 'Who put the colours in the rainbow?'

- Sally, the headteacher, welcomed everyone. Then she asked if anyone knew the last verse of the Bible. Nobody did, so Ben put it on the screen. Sally invited everyone to turn to their neighbour and greet them with the words 'May the grace of Jesus be with you today'.

- Sally then asked if anyone knew the first verse of the Bible; many did. She introduced a sketch which the children had prepared at school, based on Genesis 1.

- Roger then put everyone into groups of four. He explained that God often speaks to us directly and personally when we read the Bible, and said, from Psalm 19, that the same can happen when we contemplate God's creation. He gave a short testimony to illustrate. Then we showed a four minute film of beautiful scenes from the created world, asking God to speak to us as we watched. When the film was over the groups shared what they had heard (the children heard much more than the adults!).

- Pete took over and explained that this service was the beginning of a new pattern. He introduced the team, putting baby pictures of the team members on the screen and inviting people to guess who was who.

- Then Nicola told a story illustrated by pictures. The point of the story was that God had created each one of us differently because he has a special purpose for each one of us.

- Roger introduced Psalm 139.14 and asked the children what a womb is. One boy knew the answer. Roger explained that the Bible says God is in charge of what happens in the womb. So what did happen? There was one egg and a million sperm, and the sperm had a race, which one of them won. Roger invited a female volunteer to put on an egg costume, and then asked every man aged between 30-50 (there were about fifteen) to hold a piece of ribbon representing a sperm. We went outside and the men had a race. Darren won; his ribbon was the first to touch the egg. What the Bible says is that the race in the womb was overseen by God – Darren won because God wanted him to win. If any other sperm had won, each of us would have been a completely different person.

- Roger said that this gives us a problem; if God has made each of us to be exactly the person he wants us to be, how come we aren't perfect? Roger shared one thing that he doesn't like about himself and so did some of the other team members.

- Roger explained that what is true of him is true of everything else that God has made. The congregation identified things about the creation that are good but also things that are not so good. Roger then asked each group to consider why God made things this way?

- Several people suggested answers. Roger said that while all these answers are good, the best answer is that bad things came into the world after God had made it, and those things affect all of us. So one day God would send his Son, who would be revealed as a saviour, the one who turns bad things into good things. Lots of examples were given of the ways in which Jesus saves the world.

- We sang 'My Jesus, my saviour' and then Ben led us in a prayer.

If Mark works with a team he will find that putting together an all age service outline of this kind is quite easy.

You will see that the service outline consists of a series of short sections, on this occasion thirteen, all based on the theme. Here are some of the ways in which you can use the sections:

- Give a well illustrated short talk
- Tell a Bible story
- Help the congregation to memorise a verse of scripture
- Show a short film
- Sing a song
- Play a game
- Have a quiz

- Present a sketch
- Use puppets to teach something
- Have someone give a testimony
- Ask the congregation some questions
- Lead people in prayer
- Invite people to make a prayer of commitment
- Ask people to call out names of people or countries needing prayer
- If it fits the theme, pray for healing. It often works best to have the children lay hands on and pray for the adults
- Ask people to come to the front to do something symbolic – eg placing a stone in a water tank as a means of confession, or standing before the cross as a way of making a commitment to follow Jesus
- Speak out liturgical prayers
- Interview someone
- Ask the groups to make or draw or discuss something
- Ask the groups to share their experiences
- Ask the groups to pray for one another
- Ask the groups to listen to God and share what they heard

As you get going you will find that the team will come up with lots of other ideas.

A good biblically-based service outline is crucial to the success of an all age service, but there is more to an all age service than just a good service outline. Mark should ensure that the team is big and dedicated enough to deliver the following (these points also apply to services at which the children are taught in Sunday school for part of the time):

- An excellent welcome; each person who comes is identified and someone shows an interest in them.
- A good time for all – dads, mums, children and grandparents go home having thoroughly enjoyed themselves.
- An event which feels special to the children. This can be conveyed through the atmosphere, the songs, the way a story is told, through opportunities to pray, through a special person. But the question is did the child feel wonder, peace, mystery, fear? Have the children had an opportunity to think and talk about the purpose of their lives, their

experience of God, the question of suffering or the mystery of death? Have they been asked to use their imagination? Will they be thinking and talking about the session after it is over?

- Facilities for children aged under three, so that they can participate in the service and absorb the atmosphere in a way that is not too distracting for everyone else.

- An event which is well planned but is flexible enough to go wherever the congregation takes it. Pre-determined conclusions or responses are not as important as the feeling that everyone present becomes thoroughly engaged with the process.

- An event in which care has been taken about the space in which the event happens. What does it look and feel like? What objects are to be found in it, and what do these objects say to us? If, for all or part of the time, children meet separately from adults, the children's spaces are equally important.

- An event which promotes interaction. The children are not an audience. They must experience interaction with other children, with adults, and with God. Ask yourself 'are the children free to share their own thoughts?'

- An event led by a team of authentic Christians whose lives are rooted in prayer and who are used to praying together. The team are not placed on a rota; they provide continuity of leadership. They are as committed as they expect the children to be.

- An event which teaches a radical discipleship of the kind Jesus taught.

- Jesus is presented as alive and powerful, able to meet needs directly through answered prayer.

- A pastoral team which works the room from the first arrival to the last departure, making contact with one person after another. This team should be trained to listen, and be able to engage in deep and meaningful conversations when they spot needs. They should also know how to pray with people.

- Opportunities for creativity. Children learn by doing things; they should leave having made or performed something.

- An event which gives the children jobs to do. Involve children in setup, involve them in music and drama, in welcoming, in distributing refreshments.
- Opportunities for creativity. Children learn by doing things; they should leave having made or performed something.
- An event which gives the children jobs to do. Involve children in setup, involve them in music and drama, in welcoming, in distributing refreshments.
- An event which offers everyone the opportunity to listen for the voice of God and share what they have heard.
- An event which offers everyone an opportunity to pray for the needs of others and to learn that when we pray, we pray with the authority of Jesus and so can expect answers.
- Good food. It is best to make the standards high and the food free. Perhaps have a separate and mainly older team to prepare food.
- Administrative backup capable of creating a database with a list of all who come and their contact details as well as a good website and a Facebook group.
- Periodic social outings for everyone who belongs to the event community.
- The capability to follow up each family that comes by paying visits to their homes.

If Mark can provide all these things the event will grow in numbers and quickly become established. As numbers grow, Mark may have to increase the size of the team.

18. SUNDAY SCHOOLS – SMALL GROUPS FOR CHILDREN

Warning: Do not feed your children on a diet consisting entirely of monthly all age services. Each child (and adult) needs to also be part of a small group which meets weekly and encourages them to become disciples of Jesus.

At the beginning of this book I introduced you to Donna and Alex, the two most capable children's workers that I know. Donna and Alex each work for churches which only rarely hold all age services. Their expertise lies in running successful Sunday schools – not that Alex or Donna would call what they do a Sunday school, which sounds old fashioned!

They both prefer Sunday services at which the children are together with the adults for part of the time and in Sunday school for part of the time. This will I think normally be the best pattern for large churches like theirs. The all age part is needed for the all-important interaction between adults and children, and to make children feel part of the church as a whole and adults feel that the children matter.

But both Donna and Alex know what I have discovered from working with adults: you cannot make disciples through worship services alone. To help the children become disciples of Jesus you must also provide small groups which enable you to work with them as individuals. On Sunday children do need to feel part of the adult church, but on most Sundays they also need to learn as part of a group of children of their own age.

Sunday school teachers are given a responsibility by God and on behalf of the church for the spiritual formation of a group of children. As every parent knows, bringing up children is a matter of being consistent in the example that you give them, and then taking every opportunity to teach them, to give encouragement and praise when you can, and to correct when you must. The Sunday school teachers share this task with the children's parents.

Warning: Do not be content with a Sunday School team that works on a rota. In the short term rotas may be the only way, but the aim is to find teachers who feel called to the task and are committed enough to be there almost every week.

The aims of a good Sunday School

It is very important for the Sunday school teachers to be clear about aims. What they must long for and pray for is that each child should grow up as a disciple of Jesus. A disciple is much more than someone who knows the content of Bible stories; these stories must live in their lives.

So what exactly is a disciple of Jesus? Below is a list of aims for Sunday school teachers to work from. Children who are disciples of Jesus are children who have come to the following convictions and share in the following experiences:

- They have learned to love God's creation and wonder at it.

- They love to be the person who God has made them to be, especially the way that God has made them to be creative.

- They believe that their lives have a unique purpose.

- They have learned to acknowledge and deal with the flaws in themselves, knowing how to come to the cross and there find forgiveness and help to change.

- They have learned to acknowledge and deal with flaws in other people and flaws in the world they live in. They are able to trust God when things go wrong.

- They believe that Jesus is God, and know why they believe it.

- They have heard about the resurrection of Jesus and believe that he is alive today. They know that for themselves and for their families death will not be the end.

- They believe that Jesus has authority over sin, suffering, Satan, and death and are learning to use this authority in their own lives and the lives of others.

- They are committed to following Jesus wholeheartedly; they are learning to be honest, faithful, merciful, obedient, patient, loving, kind, and humble, because this was how Jesus was and this is what Jesus taught.

- They have received the Holy Spirit and know what it is like to be full of the Spirit.
- They exercise the gifts of the Spirit in harmony with others.
- They know what it is like to be intimate with God as Father.
- They know how to look for and find God's guidance.
- They feel themselves to be committed members of the church community.
- They have learned to enjoy praise and worship.
- They love to participate in communion and appreciate the power of the bread and the wine.
- They have learned to pray and receive answers to prayer, both on their own and with others.
- They read the Bible daily and hear God speaking through it.
- They have learned how to work hard at all they do, including their school work, not out of fear or ambition but because this pleases God.
- They have learned not to be afraid of other people, but to love and serve them.
- They are generous with money.
- They are committed to the cause of Jesus and aim every day to make disciples for him.
- They are aware of what God is doing in other countries and give their support through prayer and by raising money.

  Warning: It is vital that Sunday School teams have clear vision. The over-arching aim is to make disciples of Jesus; it is not to produce children who know Bible stories.

Working with a group of children in a Sunday school is similar to working with a class in a primary school (though usually with fewer children). Above all you need a lesson plan with detailed instructions for how to use the time.

Some teachers will be able to create their own plans but most will need these to be provided for them. Fortunately there is plenty of good material available; google 'Sunday school material' and you will find masses of stuff. The list of aims above can be used as a guide when selecting material.

> **Warning: Set high standards for your Sunday school teachers but do not leave them to work unsupported; they need help to find material, they need individual encouragement, and they need to feel part of a team which has clear vision.**

Imagine yourself to be one of Mark's Sunday school team. Each week you meet with the children and follow the lesson plan which Mark and his team leader have provided for you. Week by week you will be getting to know the children as friends and you will be praying for them.

Look again at the aims listed above. This is what you want for your children – this is what you are praying for. From time to time you are so excited because one or more of the children in your group seems to be getting it. When that happens, be very grateful to God, and full of encouragement to the children. They will learn these things at the age of three, then again at four, then again and again throughout their lives.

I once worked closely with Sarah, a Sunday school teacher in our church in Leicester. Sarah taught seven and eight year olds. Every Tuesday she had them in church for a fun activity and on Sunday she taught them in Sunday school. Sarah loved those children. I once asked her what motivated her and she said 'it is the thought of what my children will become'. Mark's team could do worse than try to be like Sarah.

19. OUTREACH EVENTS FOR FAMILIES

It may take Mark a year to establish a family worship event, or it may take two or three, but eventually he will succeed: one day there will be a critical mass of families coming regularly. Most of those families, adults and children, will be moving ahead in their discipleship. At this point, Mark needs a series of outreach events.

The natural order is to establish all age services first, then a good Sunday school, and only then make a start on outreach events; but in some circumstances a church leader might prefer to begin on the outreach events before the worship event has been thoroughly established, or even to start with outreach events.

In making his plans for outreach events Mark should not bypass the church council but, as before, go to them with a detailed proposal. He will need to show that his team is big enough to start on these new events while still continuing to run the all age services and the small groups for children to the same standard.

Outreach events are an attempt to reach out to families who are not yet part of the church community. They do not need to happen weekly. But they do need to be big when they happen, and they need to be of very high standards – a cut above the standard of normal worship events. Outreach events have to be special.

Each time you hold an outreach event, advertise it thoroughly and as widely as possible; be prepared to spend money on your advertising. Involve the whole church community in getting the publicity out; almost everyone has some contact with children. Advertise in all the local schools. Ensure that each child gets a personal invitation. Expect the families who come to the worship events to come to the outreach events as well, and to invite other families.

> **Warning: Outreach events have to reach a very high standard. For many, these events will be their first ever encounter with church, and first impressions matter. Better to do them infrequently and well than frequently and badly.**

Preparing for outreach events

Outreach events for families should always be prepared by a team, probably a slightly different one from the teams which lead all age services and Sunday school. Each team member should be given the theme for the next event and asked to come up with ideas to be shared at a team meeting.

A good outreach event has four parts: first a short gathering time in which everyone is welcomed and given something to drink; then an informal period when people move around from activity to activity as they choose; then a time when everyone is together and you have the opportunity to get your message across; and finally everyone eating together. For the informal time, you could offer craft activities, provide prayer stations, play games, provide opportunities to sit and listen to a story, run a fancy dress competition, show a short film, or provide a puppet show. Some of these activities would bear directly on the theme of the event and others would wander more widely. Then when you bring everyone together, adopt the approach which I have recommended for all age events: explore the theme through a series of short sections, some quiet, some noisy, all relevant to the topic.

> **Warning: Outreach events need big teams. First assemble your team and then launch your first event. If the team is too small the standard of the event will be too low and the series of events will fail to gain the momentum it will need.**

Themes

When choosing themes for outreach events there are a number of possibilities. One option is to choose gospel themes and use the event to present the gospel message, relying on its undoubted power to reach the heart. If you go this way here is a list of possible topics to get you going:

- God, creation and me
- What's wrong with the world?
- Who is Jesus?
- Is there life after death?

- The death of Jesus
- How to become a Christian
- The work of the Holy Spirit
- Receiving the Spirit
- Living by faith
- The meaning of baptism

The main alternative is to choose themes which attempt to take life's big issues head on. Here are some possibilities; themes like these will seem more immediately relevant to the people you hope will come to the event and so may draw a bigger crowd:

- How to be happy
- How to manage your money
- How to cope when things go wrong
- How to deal with bullies and other difficult people
- The purpose of life
- How to make relationships work at home
- How to make relationships work at school
- How to include God in your day
- Forgiveness
- Who am I?
- How to succeed in exams
- The purpose of work
- How to tell someone 'I love you'
- How to get answers to prayer
- Why do people have to die?
- Science and miracles
- How to find friends

If you choose a theme from this second list, your session will have two main aims. Firstly, to provide take-home wisdom: you want to send people home with practical ideas on some of life's biggest questions. Secondly, aim to show the relevance of the gospel to these same questions.

> **Warning: Always send people away from an outreach event having learned something new which is significant to them. Then they will come back to the next one.**

An example

Consider the theme 'How to cope when things go wrong'. There is a common sense answer: When things go wrong it is sometimes your fault, sometimes someone else's fault, and sometimes no one's fault (for example when you have an accident). If it is your fault, learn from it. If it is someone else's fault, forgive (and perhaps rebuke) them. If it is no one's fault don't let it get you down – instead count your blessings and move on, putting the bad thing that has happened behind you.

A gospel perspective suggests a fourth answer: God can bring purpose to everything, including our suffering. Jesus suffered on the cross, dying in order to save us. When we suffer in our turn, we can trust God as he did, knowing that through suffering we will find blessing. As Jesus's suffering led to life, so also, sooner or later, will ours.

Here is a sketch based on the story in Job chapter 1, in which Job handles terrible misfortune by maintaining his trust in God. The sketch aims to help people ask themselves how they would react if something were to go badly wrong for them – would they go to God for help, or would they turn away from God? For a Bible story you could use Matthew 7.24-27, where Jesus explains that the man who built his house on rock was the one who survived the storms. This can be linked to the children's story of the three little pigs; the house made from bricks was the house which kept the wolf out.

The story of Job – a sketch written for an all age event

Narrator: There was once a man in the land of Uz whose name was Job.
Job enters and everyone claps and whistles.
Narrator: Job was a very good man who never did anything wrong.
Everyone claps.
Narrator: Job loved God very much and worshipped him every day.
God enters and takes centre stage. Job bows low before God. Everyone claps.
Narrator: Because Job was so good and godly God made him very rich. He had lots of money and lots of houses and lots of children and lots of animals.
Job bows low before God. Everyone claps.
Narrator: Then Satan came to see God.
Enter Satan looking very wicked. Everyone hisses.

Narrator: God said to Satan:

God: Have you seen my servant Job?

Satan: (with resignation) Yes.

God: Isn't he wonderful?

Satan: No!

God: Yes he is. He is very good and very godly. If only everyone I made was like him.

Satan: He is only like this because you treat him so well!

God: No, he is like this because he loves me.

Satan: Let me treat him badly and then you will see.

God: Very well.

God leaves the stage and Satan takes the centre.

Satan: Now Job, we will see what happens when I get to work.

Satan laughs.

Narrator: The first messenger arrives and speaks to Job.

Enter first messenger.

1st messenger: There has been a stock market crash; all your money is gone.

Narrator: A second messenger arrives.

2nd messenger: There has been a great storm. All your houses have fallen down.

Narrator: Another messenger arrives.

1st messenger: There has been foot & mouth disease; all your animals have been put down.

Narrator: Then another messenger comes.

2nd messenger: Ebola has struck and all your family is dead.

While the messengers are speaking Satan looks extremely pleased, but Job stays serene.

Satan leaves the stage and God once again takes up his place in the centre.

Satan: Now we will see what Job will do.

Job turns to face the congregation and says:

Job: The Lord has given, the Lord has taken away. Blessed be he.

Then Job turns and bows low before God.

Satan runs away screaming.

God lifts Job to his feet and gives him a big hug.

Whatever the topic, what you have to imagine and, with God's help, actually make happen is that everyone who comes, children and adults, go away deeply challenged and encouraged because they have been given insight into some of life's most puzzling problems, and also heard something, even experienced something, of the power of Jesus to touch their lives.

An outreach event is the team's opportunity to get the message of the gospel across. Don't miss this opportunity! Study Isaiah 55.10-11, Romans 1.16, and Hebrews 4.12 – all verses which show how powerful God's message is. When you run outreach events, be determined to deliver the gospel message. Clothe yourself deliberately in his power, and be amazed at what God will do.

> **Warning: Don't fail to see that an outreach event is a 'power encounter'. Pray a lot beforehand. Get a team of people praying during the event. Expect things to happen.**

Messy Church

One good way of getting going on outreach events is to join in with the flourishing Messy Church movement first developed by Lucy Moore at St Wilfred's in Portsmouth. The Messy Church website (messychurch.org.uk) has lots of good ideas. In some places Messy Church happens on a Saturday or Sunday, with the aim of reaching out to whole families and establishing a completely new congregation. In others, Messy Church takes place after school on a weekday, reaching out mainly to mothers and children with the aim of drawing them into the regular life of the church.

Messy Church can be run in many different ways and contexts, and it provides an excellent model for reaching out to families who have no previous church experience. After a period of arrivals and welcome a Messy Church event normally begins with an hour of varied craft activities, with people of all ages moving from one another as they choose. Then everyone joins together in a time of all age worship, usually lasting fifteen minutes, at which the theme of the event is explained and explored; the earlier craft activities are all linked to this same theme. Finally the event ends with a hot meal.

Today many places are running regular Messy Church events with great success, drawing in large numbers of parents and children who are not otherwise involved with church. Messy Church is not the only way to reach out to unchurched people, but whatever style of event you choose you will be looking for a big effort from a large team. If you put in the hard work you will reap a reward.

St Mary's, Droylsden

Alison Bailie, rector of St Mary's Droylsden, has recently adopted Messy Church with great success. For some years Alison has been building good relationships with local families through contact with schools, a weekly drop-in for parents at the church school, and occasional larger events. Alison assembled a team to run Messy Church, ranging in age from teenagers to eighty year-olds and, after six months of prayer and preparation, they launched their first event in October 2012. To Alison's delight over a hundred adults and children turned up. Following the theme of 'Jesus the light of the world', everyone made lanterns and thumb pots, stained glass windows and candle cards. They decorated and ate traffic light biscuits. They enjoyed songs, a Bible story and prayers, and the session ended with a meal of hotdogs, sandwiches and cake. Subsequent events have been equally popular.

For Alison, Messy Church was not the beginning of her work amongst whole families; there was already a thriving Sunday worship event with many participating. These worshipping families provided the nucleus for the new Messy Church community.

The growth and success of Messy Church has shown us that if outreach events are done well and with imagination, it is not difficult to attract non-Christians and non-churchgoers. Most parents acknowledge that there is a spiritual side to human life, and they want their children exposed to it. Obviously this is a good thing, but there is a danger. Outreach events are very undemanding for the families who come; the danger is that people will attend when it suits them, but will never make the transition to becoming disciples of Jesus. So take courage; at every event give the invitation to take part in an enquiry group. Some may need to hear this invitation several times, but many will eventually accept it and many of those who do will become Christians. Once the Holy Spirit is on the inside of a person, priorities change and the impossible becomes possible.

Holy Trinity, St Austell

David Smith became the children's pastor at Holy Trinity, St Austell in 2012. When David arrived the weekly Sunday school consisted of five core families with a few other children who came occasionally. David wanted more, and so decided to launch a series of monthly outreach events which he calls 'parties'.
He recruited a team of fifteen people to help him with these parties, which are held every month on Saturday afternoons.

> **Warning: The best times to do outreach events are Saturday teatime and Sunday teatime. Only go for a weekday if you see no alternative.**

The first task for David was to recruit founder members for the parties. Most of the five core families were available, but he wanted more. So in the first year David ran three taster events, each aimed at making contact with and then recruiting new families for the regular monthly events. The first taster event was a light party at Halloween, which attracted twenty-four children; David followed that by a Christmas party and then an Easter party, each of which attracted forty children. David chose these occasions because they are so easy to advertise and are recognised events in the secular calendar. David and the team followed up the families that came to these events and recruited some of them as founder members of the monthly parties. From this beginning he has established a regular attendance of forty children; he has the names of one hundred children on his database.

David's parties are very similar in style to Messy Church, except that David has found that boys do not take to craft activities as readily as girls. So for the first hour he provides five games for children to play as well as five craft activities related to the theme. And he extends the worship time to last for twenty minutes. Each of the monthly parties is advertised very thoroughly. Church members are given flyers to use as invitations. The children are encouraged to invite friends, and adults bring grandchildren and invite neighbours. The events are advertised on the internet, through the local primary schools and through the church's mums and tots club. So far all of David's parties have drawn a higher proportion of non-church families than church families.

At the meal, which ends the event, David puts feedback cards on the table which include a tick-box section allowing people to indicate ways in which they could get involved in helping run future parties, or get involved in other ways in the church. From this he has already recruited five of the parents to Alpha and has added a small number of families to the Sunday morning worship event.

> **Warning: At outreach events always use feedback cards. You need this, first to create a database of the people who come, and second to recruit people to enquiry courses.**

Outreach events for parents

Once his family outreach events are established and popular, Mark could launch another kind of event, this time for mums and dads only. The best form is likely to be a meal, with a speaker who facilitates discussion and invites questions. It is not as easy to get men to come as it is women, so speakers should confine themselves to topics which fascinate men between the ages of 30 and 50. Four topics which I use a lot are 'How to raise good kids', 'Has science made God unnecessary', 'Causes and cures for stress', and 'How to make your first million'. Whatever the subject, the speaker should offer take-home wisdom and humour, but should also show the relevance of the gospel to the subject.

> **Warning: Outreach events for parents should always have young men as their main target audience. Whatever else you do, make sure that the men who come not only enjoy themselves but have their minds blown by the quality of the ideas they encounter.**

20. SMALL GROUPS FOR PARENTS

In 1967 I started my first small group for adults; there were four of us. Our emphasis was on Bible study (we studied Hebrews) and on outreach (we went from door to door in the street where I lived). We were determined to share our faith whenever we could, and we helped many to find faith, mostly from among our friends. The group grew steadily and within four years had reached seventy members; by then we had divided into several groups which usually met independently, and occasionally together. This pattern of one initial group becoming many groups has repeated itself several times over the years, most recently in Leicester where eventually six hundred and fifty people were meeting in sixty-five groups. My observation of many churches is that only those which take their small group ministry seriously see significant growth. And the church need not be large.

As I explained in Chapter 18, running small groups for children will probably mean Sunday school classes, or perhaps an extra meeting at some point during the week. But reaching families also means reaching parents, and for the parents too small groups are essential. It is in the context of small groups that most adults come to faith, and it is only in the context of small groups that adults will grow significantly in their discipleship.

> **Warning: Do not imagine that you can grow a big church without introducing a small group system. In our culture no one has ever been able to do this.**

A good way to get a small group going is to offer a course of some kind and see who comes. The course will only last for six to ten weeks, but if it goes well then those who have completed the course may express the desire to continue together on a more permanent basis.

Here are some suggestions for possible courses: [1]

- **An enquiry course** for people who have unresolved questions about the fundamentals of the Christian faith. The excellent Alpha course is the best known. An alternative is the ReSource course,

[1] See alpha.org; resource-arm.net; relationshipcentral.org.

Beyond Ourselves, which covers more ground and is more interactive. Have a look at both of these.

- **A discipleship course.** *Beyond Ourselves* is the first of ReSource's three part programme *The God who is There*, which gives a thorough and practical grounding in the basics of Christian discipleship. Any of the three books can be used as an initial course.
- **An outreach course** which teaches a group of Christians how to reach out to their friends with the gospel message. ReSource publishes an eight week course called *Beautiful Lives*.
- **A Lent course.** ReSource publishes a very helpful one called *Season of Renewal*.
- **A marriage course** for couples. The best known is from HTB.
- **A parenting course.** Also available from HTB.

I find it is best to wait until I have two or three people who would like to do one of these courses. Then I fix a start date about two months ahead and use those two months to advertise the course as widely as possible; this always brings in more people. The course might be for dads only, or mums, or for couples, or for all comers. It doesn't matter which; the main thing is to get something going.

A small group ministry usually only takes off if the church leader gets involved right from the start. So Mark should lead the first course himself, along with one or two of the team members. When the course is over he should suggest to the group that they might like to stay together and do something else. Assuming this is what happens, Mark should continue as the group leader.

Mark will find, once he gets started, that it is not difficult to grow a small group quite rapidly. The key is to start by establishing one group which meets regularly. After two or three months, try to gain new members by advertising the group at every worship and every outreach event, giving personal invitations to join the group whenever you can. New people can be added one by one, and when numbers grow big enough the group should divide into two. With this in mind Mark should be training the people who will each lead half of the group when it divides. There is no

Limit to the number of groups that could develop from this beginning.

The main limiting factor to the growth of a small group ministry is the quality of leadership. With good leadership a small group will grow and grow and eventually need to divide. With poor leadership a group will become inward looking and eventually die. As Jesus once said, 'the harvest is plentiful but the labourers are few'. Recruiting dedicated labourers has always been the key to church growth.

> **Warning: Small groups need good leadership. Do not set up groups with untrained, unsupported leaders, or with leaders who do not have time to do the job properly.**

The task of a small group leader is four-fold:

1. To run meetings which over a period of time prove to be life-changing for those who come.

2. To be a hard-working friend and pastor to each member of the group.

3. To recruit new members. Sometimes groups grow very quickly, but normally you can expect to be able to double the size of the group over two years.

4. To share the leadership of the group with at least one other person so that when the time comes the group is able to divide.

None of this is easy to achieve, and so each small group leader should be supported by a coach or mentor who is able to give encouragement and advice. No one should be left to do this job on their own.

> **Warning: Small group leaders must commit to all four parts of the task. If the meetings are unhelpful people will drop out; if the people are not pastored they will not grow; if no one new joins, the group will stagnate; if there is no assistant leader to share the work, the group leader will suffer from overload.**

21. SOCIAL ACTION PROJECTS

Jesus said to his disciples "Let your light so shine before men that they may see your good works and glorify your Father who is in heaven." Everyone knows that deeds usually speak louder than words. It is striking that Jesus says 'see your good works'; he does not say 'hear your good words'.

For Mark and his church, 'good works' means four things. First it means individual Christians visibly living lives which are based on the teaching of Jesus in the Sermon on the Mount. Secondly it means hundreds of acts of kindness shown by the church members to members of the secular community in which the church is set – the ideal church is lots of Good Samaritans going about their daily lives in the way that the original Good Samaritan went about his. Thirdly, good works means powerful prayers – Mark's church must discover how to pray as Jesus prayed, so that it becomes a place where people go when they are helpless and need divine intervention. Finally, good deeds means social action – social action is when the church acts as a whole to address a keenly felt need within the community.

Where social action is concerned, Mark has two options. One possibility is to begin his ministry to families by committing the team to a social action project of some kind. This is the right way to go if the human needs of families in his parish are crying out for attention, and if he thinks that his team is in a position to do something really significant about it. Worship events, outreach events and small groups can wait until the social action project is in full flow.

The more likely option is that Mark will decide to leave social action projects until later, when the ministry to families has become strong and new families are joining in all the time. By then Mark will have identified a need, preferably a big and obvious one that everyone agrees about, and he will be able to organise his team to do what they can to meet this need. Before starting on the new project Mark should discuss everything with the church council and get both their moral support and a budget to finance it.

In some places the most obvious need is to bring some life and colour into the community. To try and meet this need the church will put on attractive events which enable families to come together and enjoy themselves, for example a big community party or a treasure hunt or a holiday club in the summer. In places where poverty is a problem, money could be raised to support poorer families, perhaps through a food bank. In other places a marriage course or a parenting course could be offered, perhaps advertising through the schools. In some places children have nowhere to go at the end of the school day – I know of two churches in Rutland which open their doors at 3.30pm and provide a safe environment for all who come. Doing any of these things will serve to strengthen the link between the church and the community.

If the secular community is already doing some good things the church could join in. In Southampton the local council has asked the church to look for families for forty children who are awaiting adoption. So far seventy church families have expressed interest.

In my church in Leicester we were confronted every day by many homeless and rootless people. These people would come and knock at our door. We decided to welcome them, and set up the church as a drop-in centre where people could find friendship, food, warmth, and clothing every Friday and Sunday evening. Many came, and many of our church members were involved. Originally we did this entirely out of compassion but as time went by we came to realise that this highly visible activity was also earning us the respect of the community, building up our credibility, and making it much easier for us to get a hearing when we tried to put the gospel into words.

> **Warning: Churches can be made to grow without engaging in any form of social action. But only up to a point. Some people will never be reached until they see the church visibly making sacrifices for the good of the community.**

> **Warning: In most situations it is unwise to set up time-consuming social action programmes until worship, outreach, and small groups have become strong. Only once this has been done should you go for social action.**

There are probably other churches within Mark's parish that are also trying to work with children and families. Mark will want to be on good terms with the leaders of these churches, and he will want to serve them in any way he reasonably can. Mark will find that social action projects are usually a good way for churches to work together.

> **Warning: Be on good terms with other churches but do not engage in shared ministry until the family ministry in your own church is thriving; then join in as equal partners.**

St Saviour's, Branston

Mick Ellor became the vicar of Branston in 2010, at which point the church had no children and very few adults. Mick took advantage of the fact that the church building is well placed within the community and that it has an attractive grassy area outside. He decided to run a series of open-air parties for families. Crowds came and from the beginning Mick was able to make many contacts. Four years on the church is full on Sunday, including many of those families.

22. MINISTRY TO YOUNG ADULTS WITHOUT CHILDREN

Chapter 7 of this book was about targeting. I suggested that for someone like Mark who is starting more or less from scratch, the initial target group should normally be whole families. But I also mentioned six other possible target groups, and I now want to look at each of these in turn.

In Chapter 7 I gave examples of times in my own ministry when I too was starting from scratch and could have tried to work with whole families, but decided instead to put my energies into a different target group. So I am aware that some of you will have decided to do the same, preferring to take advantage of a clear opening to work, say, with mums and tots or with dads rather than with whole families. In the next few chapters we will look at these alternative options more closely.

Some of you will not be starting from scratch; your church already has a thriving ministry to whole families and your question is 'What do I do next?' Have a look at the list of target groups in Chapter 7 and choose another group. This will mean a new team, a new set of proposals for the church council and a new budget. It may also mean bringing in a new paid staff member to lead the new ministry.

The first of the other possible target groups to consider is young adults, some of whom may be married but none of whom yet have children; most of these people will be in their twenties. In some places, for example in rural areas, there will be relatively few of these people, but in others, particularly in large cities, there will be a great many.

In a city, particularly in the centre of a university city, it makes sense to target these young adults before you do anything else. If you can attract a crowd of young adults, eventually the ministry to families will take care of itself. The young adults will grow older, get married, have children, then become part of the family ministry. They will also provide leadership for the church for years to come.

Warning: If you are leading a city church do not neglect young adults (aged 18-30). These people are all around you and they have a lot of time available. Concentrate on them and they will become the foundation of your church. Neglect them and a church in a city will stagnate.

The essential principles for reaching young adults are little different from those for reaching out to any other target group. Here is a step-by-step summary of what someone in a city ministry should do:

- Get everyone in the church and the community talking about the importance and the needs of young adults.

- Decide how the new ministry will be led: by the church leader, by a paid staff member, or by a volunteer.

- If a new paid worker is to be recruited, work out how to raise funds and make a proposal to the church council.

- Once a new leader is appointed, form a core team to help run the new ministry. This team will need to be large enough, have a balance of sexes, and consist mainly of people who are in their twenties. As the team is recruited it should begin to meet for regular worship, Bible study and prayer, and for the purpose of developing vision for the coming ministry.

Recruiting this core team might happen quickly or slowly, but it should become the priority of the ministry leader until the team is in place. The way to recruit a team is to mix as much as possible with the target group and ask God to lead you to the right people.

The size of the core team will determine the eventual size of the ministry. Multiply the team size by four; this gives you a good idea of how many people will eventually be involved. If you want to be able to recruit more young people than this you will need to increase the size of your team.

Warning: Do not set out on a ministry to young adults with a team that is too small. Start your ministry by praying for and recruiting a good team.

- The team should devote themselves to making contact with the target group by whatever means possible. Then do whatever you can to turn these cold contacts into firm friendships. This will probably mean throwing lots of parties.

- Start at least one small group, led by one of the core team (probably the leader), and invite everyone you meet who belongs to the target age group to join it. Depending on how God guides you, this could be a group for Christians which aims to provide fellowship and promote discipleship, or it could be an enquiry group aimed at interested non-Christians. Ideally it would be good to have at least one group of each kind so that everyone you meet could be included somewhere.

Whatever kind of group you start, when you ask people to join be clear about what is expected of them; don't set the standards too high, but don't set them too low either; remember that if these groups are to become the foundation of your ministry, you will need to find some Faithful, Available and Teachable people.

- Once you have about twenty people involved (maybe after two years, maybe much more quickly), make a proposal to the church council for a new worship event, probably but not necessarily a new Sunday evening service in the church. This event can also be used to target teenagers. Older people will be welcome at the new event but must not be allowed to determine way the event works, for example in the choice of music.

- Before you launch the event, share your vision for it as widely as possible within the target group (young adults). As you share with people listen carefully to their advice on how to turn the vision into reality; especially ask people about the content of the event and the timing (is Sunday the best day?).

- Launch the event, but only when you can deliver excellent teaching, inspiring worship, powerful prayer ministry, a capable pastoral team, and a good time for all. Do not get started in a space which is too big – plan to move when numbers increase. Twenty people meeting in a café somewhere can become the nucleus from which a much bigger event can grow.

- Once your worship event has become established, plan and launch a new event – this time a bi-monthly outreach event for both Christians and non-Christians. The outreach event could either replace the now normal weekly worship event, or it could take place on a different day of the month. Each time you run the outreach event, give it maximum publicity. Make sure you can deliver it to a very high standard, and before you start make sure you have enough founder members.

- Once the outreach event programme has started look for three people from the target group who are not yet Christians and would like to take part in an enquiry group. Set a start date for about a month ahead, and use this month both to develop a strong relationship with the three and also to advertise the enquiry group as widely as possible. When the enquiry course is over, form the group members into a discipleship group and then start another enquiry group. Ask one of your team to lead the new group.

You will find that the weekly worship event and the bi-monthly outreach event will provide you with a steady stream of people who are ready for enquiry courses. If you are able to keep adding people to your team then there will be no limit to growth. One group will eventually become many.

- When you judge the time is right, involve everyone who comes to the worship event, the outreach event, or belongs to a small group to join in a social action project which aims to make a significant difference to the lives of people in the area. (This might happen after perhaps four years).

- Form links with churches in the area which have a similar ministry. Social action projects work well when two churches work together. For example healing on the streets (healingonthestreets.com) if done together is good for all the churches involved and also good for the community. Another ministry which works well with this age group is street pastors (streetpastors.co.uk).

  Warning: If you have a large number of young people living in your catchment area (this will be so in any city) do not set your sights too low. If you persist and are patient, if you train your people properly, if you keep the vision clear, you can expect to eventually have 5% of these people in your church; and 5% of a lot is a lot.

23. MINISTRY TO DADS

All the evidence suggests that if the father of a family becomes a Christian then his family usually follows. On the other hand if you win mother and children it is only rarely that you win the father as well. This leads some to argue that it is more important to target dads then to target families.

I have some sympathy with this argument. For example I am in touch with James, a vicar from the south coast. James's churches are doing just a little better than Mark's churches. But recently James has had a slice of unusual good fortune – or perhaps God has been answering his prayers. In the space of a few months no fewer than six young men, all of them fathers, have moved into his area and joined his church. And all of them seem quite keen to learn. My advice to James has been to prioritise these six men above all else. If they become committed disciples of Jesus, the church has a bright future; what they find, their families will also find. James should concentrate on the dads!

To get his group of dads James has had to do no work – they just turned up. The same might happen for Mark, but until it does he is wise to continue to target families, but in a way that makes it likely that dads will want to join in. This means organising his ministry along the following lines:

- Mark should include men in his core team, including some who are also dads. If the core team only has women, men are much less likely to join in.

- When the new worship or outreach events get going, the male team members should be given the task of welcoming and making friends with any new men who come.

- Design the events so that the men who come are not required to just sit and listen. Men need interaction, both with each other and with the children. Men also need roles.

- Time the events to suit men, bearing in mind that young men are normally available only at the weekend or in the evening.

- Provide excellent food for the events – the kind of food which men enjoy. For example bacon butties at breakfast are always a winner!

Warning: In choosing a team to work with families, aim for a balance of the sexes. The same is true for any other group in your church except those that are specifically for women.

If he does these things the day will come when Mark has a group of dads who are coming reasonably regularly to the events. Once this happens he should try to band these men together.

I did this myself over many years and it worked well. I decided to ask the men in my church who had children to meet up with me once a week. I invited them personally and individually, and most said yes. I did not invite them until I had got to know them well. If they don't know you they will probably say no.

I was tough about who could come to my dads' group. If you want a group for dads, it's important not to allow older men to come – this may not be popular, but the fact is that young men do not join groups which are dominated by older men. Next I didn't allow anyone to join if they would not agree to aim for 100% attendance and guarantee 70%. Men are men – they understood and respected these conditions. The dads who came to that meeting became my long-term close personal friends.

Warning: In setting up a dads' group set high standards for attendance right from the start. Once attendance starts becoming irregular the whole thing will fail.

When you meet, keep it short; men are busy. Meet for food – breakfast is good especially if it is on a Saturday. Lunch times during the week will work for many men. When you meet, pray together and share something from the scriptures which is very practical. Make sure the session is highly interactive.

To this weekly meeting add an outreach programme. Again breakfast on Saturday may be the best time, though when I have done this myself we always had evening meetings, beginning with a good meal.

The dads brought other dads. The meetings always had a good speaker and the subjects were always practical and life-based. This produced takers for enquiry courses and this in turn produced conversions. This would work anywhere. All you need is an initial group of Christian young men.

Then add a fun programme. For example any kind of regular sports programme will be popular. Our group enjoyed a regular football game in the local park. There are of course many other possibilities.

In Chapter 11 I described the Tea Time service which Rob and Marilyn Thomas have begun in Trowbridge. Already this service is attracting several young men who come with their children and join in happily. Rob would be wise to make these young men the absolute priority of his time, making friends with them and aiming to bring them into a little enquiry group – probably not a full-blown Alpha course but something short, simple and practical. If he is successful at bringing the dads to faith and banding them together, the long term success of the church's family ministry is assured.

Churches are for men, women and children. Throughout my ministry I always prioritised spending time with men, with the result that we always had as many men as women among our church members. Women are often more available than men, and more naturally drawn to the church; this makes it all the more important for a church leader to spend as much time as possible working with men.

> **Warning: If you are a male church leader and your church has any men under fifty, make these men the priority of your time; if you are female church leader, find a lay man who would be willing to invest his time in such men. Go out of your way to make close friendships. Aim to disciple these men and to band them together. Neglect this opportunity and you are missing your greatest chance to build a significant church.**

24. MINISTRY TO PRIMARY AGE CHILDREN

The next target group to consider is children aged between four and eleven. Choosing this group means aiming not at families but specifically at children; parents will not normally stay for the activities. A church which already has a thriving ministry to families may find that opening children's clubs of this kind will create an excellent context for reaching out to other children and other families.

> **Warning: Do not open clubs for children until Sunday provision f or families at your church is already strong. A children's club will use up resources that are needed elsewhere.**

To start up a club for children you will need a good leader and a good team (one team member for every four children), an agreed budget and some founder members. It is much easier to recruit founder members if there are already children attending a family worship event; they will bring their friends and numbers are likely to increase quite rapidly.

Allow your founder members to select the best time and place for the new event. Options include school premises at lunch time or after school, or elsewhere after school or at weekends. If the school is available it is usually the best place. In Leicester we started an after-school club in a local primary school. We had no founder members at all (this was a mistake), but even so ninety children came in that first week. Supported by the head, all we did was advertise through the school.

> **Warning: Successful schools work is always built on a good relationship between the church leader and the head teacher. So if you want to work in schools first give time to this relationship.**

If the club is to last for more than an hour, it is best to begin with recreation (refreshments, games, craft activities). But it is rarely effective to make the activity purely social. It is important for the children to enjoy themselves, but it is best to follow recreation with worship and a gospel message. For this, children and team may come together in a single group, with a front-led session including contributions from team members (see the principles given in Chapter 17 for leading all age worship).

For the rest of the time children can be divided into age-groups, each with a team member in charge (this part of the session can be run in a similar way to a good Sunday school – see Chapter 18). Because most of the children will not be from Christian homes, the session themes should be chosen as if for outreach events (examples are given in Chapter 19). The children should periodically be given an opportunity to make a commitment to Jesus, with appropriate follow up and perhaps confirmation classes.

Special events can be added to the normal weekly club meetings – for example a summer holiday club, Christingle service, Exploring Easter event, Mothering Sunday, Halloween light party, bonfire party, pet service, or family treasure hunt.

The parents of the children are important, especially the ones who are not part of any church. Make friends with them and let them know what you are trying to do for their children. From time to time (perhaps once a term) have a session to which parents are specially invited. When the parents arrive, ask the children to serve refreshments, and then ask the parents to join in with what is otherwise a normal session of the club.

Discipline can be a problem in children's clubs. It is important to take a firm line with children who are disruptive by being prepared to first warn them and then, if there is no response, to exclude them. If you don't do this then you will find that the children who want to learn will stop coming and you will be left only with the disruptive ones.

> **Warning: Do not set up the children's club in a school unless you have some children in your church. Otherwise you will find that the club members, even those who come to faith, will almost never make the transition from the club to the church; and neither will their parents.**

25. MINISTRY TO SECONDARY AGE CHILDREN (YEARS 6-9)

The next target group to be considered is children aged ten to fourteen. This is not yet an issue for Mark; so far he has no children in this age group. Sooner or later though, if Mark's ministry to whole families flourishes, some of the children in those families will move into this age group. What should be done then?

If there are only two or three children, it is quite easy. If these children are aged ten or eleven it is not necessary to cater for them separately; they can be included in what you are providing for the younger children: the all age worship and outreach events, and the Sunday school. Once the children reach the age of twelve, they can be invited to form part of the core team which plans and leads all these activities. This is asking them to grow up quickly; but experience shows that as long as they are looked after carefully they will rise to the responsibility.

This will work with two or three children, but not with more. Once Mark has several older children, he would be wise to develop a new ministry focussed on their particular age group. This will require a new team; to start with a team of two will do, but as numbers grow Mark will need one leader for every six children – enthusiasts who are prepared to commit to the children for some years ahead. In this ministry continuity matters.

The new group will meet at the same time as the family ministry, but in a separate room or better still a separate building. What matters is that the children feel that they have grown up and moved on. So the new ministry needs to feel quite different to the old one.

> **Warning: As the children grow older, think ahead. As soon as family ministry has started, plan to begin a separate ministry to secondary age children. Do not expect twelve-year-olds to be happy with a ministry aimed at seven-year-olds.**

Once the new ministry is established, children may graduate to it once they reach Year 6, the last year of primary school. If they have a great time at church in Year 6 they will be ready to continue in Year 7 – otherwise they may drop church as soon as they change schools.

This ministry will almost always start with just a small group – between three and ten children. In this group, aim above all to show the children that a relationship with Jesus really works. Teach them to pray and expect answers, and to pray for each other. And teach radical discipleship which challenges them to live every day as committed disciples of Jesus. Above all aim to build their faith; this is best done by providing a series of faith challenges. They need to learn from experience that if they trust God, it works.

At this age it is helpful for the children to be mentored by one of the team. Every child is worthy of individual attention, but if this is not practicable it is best to prioritise young people who have the potential for future leadership. These are the criteria to consider:

- Someone who already shows a commitment to personal spiritual growth
- Someone who already displays courage
- Someone who is enthusiastic
- Someone who is servant-hearted, shown by volunteering for small tasks
- Someone who has people ability, shown either in a caring heart or in the ability to draw others to themselves.

Mentoring means meeting up regularly, perhaps monthly, for about an hour. It's important to be clear from the start why you are meeting and what you both hope to gain from it. Same sex mentoring works best, meeting in a location where you can be observed but not overheard (cafés are good). Make sure that appropriate safeguarding guidelines are being followed, and that the parents know what you are doing.

Here are some of the things that you may be doing in the mentoring sessions:

- Reading the Bible together
- Praying and identifying answers to prayer
- Sharing how things are going in your lives
- Preparing a group session which you will lead together
- Setting goals
- Explaining leadership principles
- Issuing appropriate challenges

In between sessions pray regularly for the person you are mentoring.

> **Warning: When working with this age group, mentoring the children is very important, but it has to be done carefully. Think about how it looks, especially to the parents. Make sure that the team members who do the mentoring are well trained.**

Alongside this individual mentoring, you will want to be thinking ahead, encouraging the children to develop a vision for a much larger group which they will help to found. Discuss with them how this can be achieved. When would the larger group meet, and where? What would the activities be? Who could you try to get involved? How could the new event be launched? How could it be advertised?

The initial group of children then become the founder members for the new event. In Leicester we opted for a Friday evening on church premises, starting at 6.30pm. In Wells we opted for a Tuesday lunchtime club at the local secondary school. In both places, once we had six children coming regularly it was not difficult to grow the numbers quite quickly, because enthusiastic children of this age are usually very good at bringing their friends.

For this age group the environment of the event makes a huge difference. It is said to take a child of this age just thirty seconds to decide whether the event is something they can commit to or not, and this depends primarily on how things look. So it's worth investing time and money on creating an attractive environment. Provide a tuck shop, pool tables, games consoles, and art and craft activities. Pay attention to the lighting and the music, and introduce drapes to make the room look special.

Warning: When working with this age group be prepared to spend time and money getting the set-up right.

When it comes to the planning of the time, it works best to spend the first half of the event on fun activities and the second half on spiritual activities – which should also be fun – bearing in mind that at this age girls usually like one thing and boys another. The YFC material Rock Solid and RS2 is very good if you have a mixture of churched and unchurched young people – and it includes advice on both activities and teaching, leaving the leaders free to focus on building relationships.

Worship seems to be less important for this age group than for the younger or older ones. But if you can provide worship led by a band of 13-18 year olds this always pays dividends. The older children will serve as role models for the younger ones.

Warning: When working with this age group always provide alternative activities – one aimed at girls and the other at boys.

One significant difference in working with this age group, as opposed to primary age children, is that whereas with the younger children the input has to come largely from the team, it is now essential to trust the children themselves to provide much of the input. Sessions should often be led by the children, initially in partnership with older team members. You will find that some are soon able to produce excellent material independently. If you fail to trust the children in this way, you will soon lose them. Once they are in Year 9 they need to be part of the team, and included in all the planning and decision making.

Warning: When working with the 11 to 14 age group, do not allow the children to become passive. They will only stick with you if you trust them and give them opportunities to lead, make decisions, and be on team.

26. MINISTRY TO SECONDARY AGE CHILDREN (YEARS 10-13)

Once children reach Year 10 they need to move on again. If you do not provide for this you will lose them. There seems to be some evidence that in rural areas children in years 6-13 can sometimes be held together in one group, but no evidence that this can be done in cities. On Sundays a few of these older children will be willing to be thought of as adults and will happily join in with what the adults are doing. And some will be happy to work as team members in a ministry to younger children. But for most it will be necessary to start another new activity aimed specifically at this age group. As before, Mark will need a good team with a new leader, and he will need founder members.

> **Warning: Do not think you can have a single ministry which covers the age group 11 to 18, for if you do you will quickly lose everyone who is over 15. For some reason this is usually less of a problem in rural areas.**

In Mark's case we are thinking years ahead, probably ten years ahead. Whether Mark is still there or not, one day his church will find itself with a bunch of teenagers; and when that day comes they must be ready. How can Mark form these teenagers, whom his team has been nurturing for years, into the springboard for a new youth ministry?

The best people to be on a youth team are the teenagers themselves, so the new leader's first job will be to invite them to join his team. This team could usefully have one other person who is not a teenager, but no more than that. Once formed, the team should begin to meet together for regular worship, Bible study and prayer, and for the purpose of developing vision for their coming ministry.

The target group for this team is teenagers: all the teenagers in the town, whether they are churched or unchurched. The first task for the team is to begin to make contact. As the team itself mostly consists of teenagers this is not difficult. The team should run lots of one-off events, varying from social events to ones at which the gospel is preached.

These events will create opportunities to reach out to new people. Teenagers are looking for friendships. They love to discuss and to argue. They are very open to the things of the Spirit, so they need to discover that the team believes in the presence of God and the power of prayer. Teenagers are quite easy to recruit to enquiry groups – Youth Alpha works well, as does *Beyond Ourselves*, published by ReSource. All of this should result in a community of teenagers who are connected, even if only loosely, to the team and to the church.

Eventually the goal of the team will be to launch a new weekly regular event, if possible on a Sunday evening; this event will become the teenagers' way of doing church. Friday or Saturday evenings are alternatives. As ever, it is important to launch the event only when you have recruited enough founder members, and in a space that fits the size of the group. Until then concentrate on evangelism and on running good team meetings.

In our church in Leicester we eventually ran the teenage work over two evenings. On Saturday the evening began with recreation and then divided into small groups, sometimes fellowship groups, sometimes enquiry groups. On Sundays most of the teenagers came to the evening service which was targeted both at them and the 18-30 age group. This service should ideally provide a stirring message, worship led by a youth band and an opportunity for prayer ministry. This is a common pattern in a large city church, but it would be a long time before a smaller church like Mark's could hope to have something this ambitious.

Once we had established Saturday and Sunday evenings with large numbers of teenagers, we felt it was time to go back to having an emphasis on evangelism, so from time to time we replaced the Saturday evening programme by an outreach event from which we were able to recruit new people to join enquiry groups. Outreach events take a lot of planning and are heavily dependent on Christian teenagers inviting their friends.

Finally, once everything else is in place, the team should be very ambitious and go for the social action option. Make contact with the teenagers living in your area, try to understand what is needed in their lives and, if it is not provided by the community already, then try to provide it.

> **Warning: Ministry to people aged between 14 to 18 should be mostly led by the teenagers themselves, with a small number of adults to guide them. This is where you train leaders for the future. To have older youth leaders taking all the responsibility is counterproductive.**

27. MINISTRY TO MOTHERS WITH PRE-SCHOOL CHILDREN

I observe that in many places ministry to mothers with pre-school children has been chosen as a starting point for family ministry. This often results in a strong mother and toddler club, but it seems also to result in a very weak ministry to whole families. The church looks strong on Tuesday morning, but on Sunday the average age remains worryingly high. Furthermore, the young mothers do not stay in the mother and toddler club for long. They are soon back to work and their children off to school, and then, because the family ministry in the church is not strong, the church loses touch with them, and very little has been gained.

This is not of course always true. Every situation is unique and every team is different. God may lead you very clearly into contact with a group of keen mums with babies who are desperate to get together, and indeed if these mums are also Christians and part of the church already you will not want to discourage them! But be aware that if this is all you do, it may be all you ever do.

So what should a new church leader like Mark do? If there is already a mother and toddler club, he or she should keep it going, but the priority should be on starting a ministry to whole families. When the time comes to recruit founder members for this new ministry, past and present members of the mother and toddler club will be the first people to talk to. Once the family ministry is going well, this and the ministry to mothers of young children will reinforce each other.

As it happens Mark's churches do not have a mother and toddler club, and I would not advise him to start one. But once the ministry to whole families is established it may well be a good thing for Mark to open a mother and toddler club in addition. The club then becomes part of the outreach from the family worship event.

So let's suppose that Mark's team decide, either as a starting point but more probably at a later stage, to start a regular mother and toddler activity. The usual caveats apply; they should not start until they have a sufficient team and a nucleus of founder members with whom they have discussed every detail – especially the question of when and where. Nor should they start until they are sure that they can do it really well. To do this they will want to be able to provide:

- A time that is really enjoyable
- Good equipment
- Good activities
- Good music
- A good talk
- People with listening skills who are able to engage with those present throughout the session
- Time to build good friendships with those who come

It is rare to find a mother and toddler club that provides all of these.

The primary aim of many mother and toddler groups, even church-based groups, is to meet the social needs of the mothers. Often there is no message and the music, if any, is secular. Such groups provide a valuable service, but this rather limited motivation will not be a good way forward for Mark. Mother and toddler clubs draw in non-Christians very easily, so why not take advantage of this?

It is best if mother and toddler clubs are set up from the start with three aims: they should provide the opportunity for mothers and children to worship together, they should aim to share the gospel with the mothers, and they should aim to provide for their social needs.

> **Warning: Do not allow a mother and toddler group which is merely social. You have limited resources, so use them to do as Christians did from the beginning – aim to spread the gospel and grow the Kingdom.**

At a mother and toddler club the talk, lasting no more than 5 minutes, should be aimed at the mothers and not the children. The person who speaks must be confident in the power of the gospel and able to present it in an interesting and relevant way. Here is a list of twenty possible topics:

1. What can we teach our children about the meaning of life?
2. When your child says 'Who made the world', what do you say?
3. The summit of God's creation – your child
4. Can we teach our children to connect with God?
5. Why is your child naughty?
6. Why is the world such a mess?
7. Who did Jesus claim to be?
8. Miracles! What to do if your child is sick
9. Jesus, the greatest teacher in the world
10. When your child gets to be 100, what then?
11. Why Christians believe in the resurrection of Jesus
12. Why did Jesus die?
13. What is forgiveness?
14. The battle between good and evil
15. A Christian is someone who believes in Jesus
16. A Christian is someone who has decided to follow Jesus
17. A Christian is someone who has Jesus in their heart
18. How to become a Christian
19. Who or what is the Holy Spirit?
20. How to receive the Holy Spirit

When you give the talk, refer to the children all the time and use them to illustrate what you are saying. It works well to follow the talk by offering a craft activity for the children, linked to the theme.

Also during the club meeting, the group can learn and enjoy Christian songs, especially action songs; the mothers can learn to say simple prayers with and for their children; those who are ill or in trouble can be prayed for. Expect miracles and they will happen! Pray for and expect that the whole session will be infused with the gentle presence of the spirit of Jesus.

During the session the team should move round the room listening sympathetically to what is going on in the lives of the mothers. They will find that in time they are having many conversations about the gospel.

If your team is strong enough and numerous enough to do all this well you will find the activity becoming increasingly popular. Once it has become established the following additional activities can be considered:

- Start a father and toddler activity on a Saturday morning. Mark Glover began an activity of this sort at Hoole Baptist Church in Chester. The event, entitled 'Who let the dads out?' was very successful, and has been copied in many places.

- Provide a programme of social activities for couples to enjoy without their children. Mix this with the occasional meal with a speaker who will bring a gospel message but one that is very relevant to family life.

- Start a marriage course for couples.

28. MINISTRY TO MOTHERS AND PRIMARY AGE CHILDREN

The issues raised by ministry to mothers and primary age children are similar to those raised by mother and toddler clubs. These ministries are always valuable, but they are rarely the place to start. Most churches have limited resources, and these are best used for an activity which involves fathers as well as mothers and children.

If your weekend ministry to whole families is flourishing, then you could consider opening a new activity, probably after school, aimed at mothers and primary age children. Once the children from your mother and toddler club start school, this will provide something for them to move on to. Both of these activities then become outreach projects from the weekend worship event.

The principles for running after-school outreach events are exactly the same as for any other outreach event (see Chapter 19), except that the people in your team, like the other adults that come to the event, will those who are available during the day – so probably very few men.

IN CONCLUSION

In Chapters 22-28 we have looked at the various options for targeting groups other than whole families – either because this seems to be the best initial way forward in your context, or (more usually) as a way of building on a family ministry which has now been successfully established. In the Appendix which follows, we take a step back and look at what you might do if your church is not yet sufficiently spiritually healthy to embark on the development of a ministry to families: these are the steps you can take to prepare the ground and ensure that it is. The appendix is followed by a list of books and resource materials you may find useful.

APPENDIX

A brief outline which explains how Mark can work to renew the church community

This section picks up from the material in Chapter 1, 'Start from where you are'. Bearing in mind that a church leader should initially focus on the existing congregation, even if that congregation has no families at all, this appendix summarises the steps that he or she should take to make friends with the people and bring new life to the church. These steps are as follows:

1. Begin by calling the church to pray
2. Revitalise the main Sunday services
3. Introduce small fellowship groups or strengthen existing ones
4. Introduce a regular outreach event
5. Start small groups for enquirers
6. Unite the church behind a social action project
7. Pay attention to the church finances
8. Look at the church website and noticeboards

   Warning: The steps in the list that follows are all essential. Do not neglect to do any of this. All of it will require patience and courage – press on slowly and steadily and get it all done. You will not regret it.

Step 1 is to call the church to pray. Mark should make it clear from the very start that he believes in the power of prayer, and he should invite the church people to pray with him, perhaps monthly, perhaps weekly, perhaps through an infrequent whole day of prayer – whatever it takes to get as many people as possible praying together.

Do not take this to the church council as a proposal; just announce it from the front, explaining that you need to pray and you would really appreciate it if others could spare the time to support you.

Maybe very few people will come to the prayer meetings. Don't worry – some will come, and their prayers will make all the difference. Find a way to pray that your people are comfortable with and always express your appreciation that they took the trouble to be there. Mention this prayer meeting frequently and let it be widely known how important it is for you.

Step 2 is to revitalise the main Sunday services. To get started, Mark should introduce the subject of Sunday services at the church council meetings, and ask members what they value in the present services and what they would like to see done differently. Mark will seek consensus, but he will not give way if this does not emerge – the most important thing is that people should feel heard. These are the reforms Mark should aim for:

Pastoral – Each member of the congregation must learn from experience that they matter. Mark should make sure that he knows everyone, and has visited and if possible entertained everyone. Mark cannot do all the pastoral work himself, so he will need to choose pastoral teams for each church and give them some training.

Ideally Mark needs one pastoral team member for every five people in the congregation, and at least one for every ten. The pastoral team members should be trained to do three things:

- When the congregation meets, Mark and the other pastoral team members will try to connect with each person, giving a particular welcome to any newcomers.

- The pastoral team is above all a listening team and will expect to have some significant and personal conversations, sometimes ending in a time of prayer. They will provide ongoing care to any congregation members who need support or encouragement.

- The pastoral team should be aware of who is missing and where appropriate make contact within a few days.

Preaching – Mark should preach well prepared, biblically based sermons which have clear relevance to the daily lives of the congregation. In time he must expect the same from those with whom he chooses to share the pulpit. This last objective will probably require both time and courage, and the more parishes that an incumbent has to cope with the harder it will be. No church can grow without good preaching.

Mark will probably find that the church has someone who has been used to being trusted with sermons, but who is not preaching well. There are dangers in challenging such a person too soon – Mark would be wise to wait for a year before facing up to the uncomfortable but necessary conversation. He must be determined that in the medium term this person will either receive help or else be persuaded to give up preaching altogether.

> **Warning: Many churches have a few dominant and difficult people. Don't let these people get you down. Be very nice to them but do not give in to them. Remember that the longer you stay the easier it will get to deal with these people. Sometimes such a person will choose to leave, and this may be the best solution.**

Sacraments – Mark's aim should be to reach a time when the congregation expects to meet with God each time they come to church. The Eucharist is central to this experience. So Mark should offer teaching on the meaning and power of the sacraments; many congregations experience the sacraments in a way that is merely ritualistic. Mark should also explain the ministry of laying on of hands, and make this available on Sunday to everyone who wishes it.

Intercessions – Mark will aim to see strong intercessory prayer, and will choose and train a team to lead this time well. The intercessions should aim to be much more than a prayerful summary of what is reported in the media. God cares for the whole world and so should we, but something is wrong if the intercessions fail to touch on the needs of the congregation, the vision of the local church and the concerns of the local community. Above all the intercessions should be upbeat, full of faith; they should be prayers which expect God to respond.

Music – It is good for a congregation to sing hymns and spiritual songs in praise of God, and when a congregation sings from the heart then everyone is uplifted. A lot, therefore, hangs on who is choosing and leading the music. What Mark wants in the long term is a good friendship with the music leaders so that he can work closely and harmoniously with them.

In some churches this will be possible right from the start. But Mark may find he has a group of musicians who are conservative and resistant to change. If so, he would be wise to say nothing much in the first year, but to tackle the problem with determination after that. It is wise to make sure the congregation knows that you love them before you sack the organist! But if the musicians are not willing to embrace change, there may be no alternative but to ask them to stand down.

Service books and news sheets – these should be attractively designed, written in accessible language and easy to use even for someone who is new. If this is not so, it's something you can change quite rapidly – most people will be very pleased.

Notices – Mark will wish the notices to reflect the vision of the congregation, so that all the activities of the church can be seen to flow from a shared and agreed purpose. The notice slot, properly used, offers a valuable opportunity to create unity.

Buildings – Mark should aim for the day when the buildings are fit for purpose and have warmth, light, and cleanliness, good facilities and technology, and high quality notice boards both inside and outside. This will cost time and money; the key is to set targets and help the church council work enthusiastically to reach them.

Refreshments – these should be provided at every service, and to a high standard.

Children – Mark hopes that increasing numbers of children will become part of the church. At this stage he needs to ensure that if a few children do come they will leave having had a good time.

Leadership – Some lucky church leaders find that they have only one church building to worry about. Others have to look after six or more churches, particularly in rural areas, and this necessitates shared leadership. Small rural congregations can be deeply conservative, but they are not unrealistic. They know that the most they can hope for is an occasional visit from their incumbent, and that the other services will be taken by a variety of others including lay readers and retired priests. They also know that where there is no leadership there is usually no vision; you cannot lead a congregation if you only see them once a month.

The best solution is to have a lay leader for each congregation. He or she may never preach a sermon or lead a service, but will always give the welcome and the notices. This person will lead the pastoral team and be responsible with the minister and the church council for developing vision. Ministers with several churches are wise to explain this to each church, and then help them to choose leaders. The minister must find time to give training, encouragement and support to each appointed leader.

Step 3 is to establish a small group system so that those who wish to find a deeper fellowship can do so. It is essential that good leaders be appointed to lead these groups, and it is often best to start with just one group initially; Mark should lead this group himself. Additional groups can then be led by people who have been part of the initial group.

If the church already has some small groups Mark should start another one as soon as possible and lead it himself. He should also arrange to visit the existing groups about once a month, though he should not try to reform them.

Mark's own group will set the standards. He should invite people to join his own group only if he feels confident that they will be faithful to the group and come more or less every week, and that they will trust him. The group meetings should have four parts:

1. Begin with welcome. Ice breakers are good, or you could just share news. This first section will normally last for about 20 minutes.

2. Then move into Bible study. Ideally this will based on the same material that was used for the previous Sunday's sermon. About 40 minutes for this is best.

3. Then move into a time of prayer and worship. Any style is fine, so long as it is agreed that the group will try to be open before God. Allow 20 minutes for this.

4. Finally talk about your daily lives. For example each week one of the group could explain what they do all day and answer questions. Then you could pray for the people who are being touched by that member's life. Allow 20 minutes for this: 100 minutes in all.

Step 4 is to introduce a regular outreach event aimed at the friends and neighbours of the congregation. This event will be organised along the following lines:

- **Venue** – The event will be held in the best available venue. This could be the church building itself but other alternatives should be considered. Guests must be made to feel that they are coming to somewhere special.

- **Frequency** – These events should be of the highest possible standard and this should limit their frequency. Perhaps initially Mark should aim for just three or four events each year. These events could be linked to the annual calendar and made to coincide with Easter, Harvest, Christmas, Remembrance etc.

- **Publicity** – Invitation cards for the outreach events should be given to each church member, who is then asked to invite anyone they know who is not yet part of the congregation.

- **Refreshments** – Aim to provide outstanding refreshments; a good meal is ideal.

- **Message** – The event should contain a message which has clear relevance to the lives of the guests and be expressed in their language. This message should also contain an explanation of the Christian gospel.

- **Fun** – The event must be fun for those who come. If guests like music, provide music. If they like quizzes, have a quiz. If they enjoy playing games, play games.

- **A way forward** – always offer guests a way forward. To this end Mark should be ready to provide an enquiry course which they can join.

Step 5 is enquiry groups. Once Mark has got going on outreach evenings he will soon find people who are not yet Christians but want to explore faith.

Step 6 is social action. Mark should not attempt this until steps 1 to 4 are in place. The congregation will have been learning through sermons and small groups that the purpose of their lives is to live for the glory of God and the good of others. They will have been learning to do this through ordinary daily living. But the time will come when Mark can establish at least one project involving the whole church which will provide a significant service to the surrounding community.

Step 7 is to make sure that church finances are strong. This can be done in the following ways:

- Each year at the final church council meeting set a budget for the coming year which balances income and expenditure. This budget should plan for an annual increase in income of 10-15%. Mark should explain to the church council that an increase of this kind is a necessary step of faith.

- Include in the budget an item for charitable giving (to the community and/or to needs overseas). This charitable giving should be gradually increased until it reaches at least 15%.

- Resolve together to stop all fundraising activities which are aimed at outsiders. The community must discover that the church is there to give to them, and not them to the church.

- As soon as you can, include in the budget an item for administrative support which will allow you to set up an office and employ someone to run it.

- At the beginning of the financial year place this budget before the congregation (both on Sundays and by letter) explaining the reasons for the increase in expenditure. At the same time preach about giving and about the godly use of money.

- Explain how tax can be recovered through gift aid, and set up a system.

- Throughout the year monitor both income and expenditure. If income dips, alert the congregation and ask them to pray.

Step 8 is to improve the website and internal and external noticeboards. Advertising matters in all walks of life. Many people now form their first impression of a church from its website. The same applies to the external noticeboards – take a look at yours and ask whether you would try out the church on the basis of what you see there. Internal noticeboards are also important; they provide an opportunity to communicate the vision of the church. If necessary redesign the noticeboards so that they communicate your vision.

Summary

If Mark takes all of the above steps this will occupy him very fully in the first two years of his ministry. He will be hoping and praying that by the end of these two years the church will have become a strong base from which they will be able to strike out together in a new direction. This new direction will be a ministry to younger people, probably to families.

USEFUL BOOKS

Adams, Kate, B Hyde & R Wooley: *The Spiritual Dimension of Childhood*, Jessica Kingsley 2008

All God's Children? Children's Evangelism in Crisis – Report, General Synod Board of Education and Board of Mission, CHP 1991

Beckwith, Ivy: *Postmodern Children's Ministry: ministry to children in the 21st century*, Zondervan 2004

Brierley, Peter: *Reaching and Keeping Tweenagers*, Christian Research 2003

Bunge, Marcia: *The Child in Christian Thought and Practice,* Eerdmans 2001

Butler, Paul: *Mega Top Tips on Offering the Best Children's Ministry,* Scripture Union 2011

Chester, Mark: *Who Let The Dads Out,* Barnabas 2012

Copsey, Kathryn: *From the Ground Up: understanding the spiritual world of a child,* Barnabas 2005

Fung, Raymond: *The Isaiah Vision – An ecumenical strategy for congregational evangelism,* WCC Publications 2002

Gardner, Jason: *Mend the Gap – can the Church reconnect the generations?* IVP 2008

Griffiths, Mark: *Don't tell cute stories – change lives!,* Monarch 2003

Griffiths, Mark: *One Generation from Extinction*, Monarch 2009

Harding, Nick: *Boys, God, and the Church: how churches can help boys grow in faith and why they do not*, Grove Books 2007

Haynes, Brian: *Shift - What it takes to Finally Reach Families Today*, Group Publishing 2009

Hilborn D & M Bird (eds): *God and the Generations – youth, age and the Church today*, Paternoster Press 2002

Hubbard, Richard: *Taking Children Seriously – developing a children's ministry in your church*, Harper Collins 1991

Hyde, Brendan: *Children and Spirituality – searching for meaning and connectedness*, Jessica Kingsley 2008

Jutila, Craig: *Children's Ministry in the 21st century: the encyclopaedia of practical ideas*, Group Publishing 2006

Kirk, Daphne: *Reconnecting the Generations*: Kevin Mayhew 2001

Kuhrt, Stephen: *Church Growth through the full Welcome of Children,* Grove Books 2009

Leach, Chris & John: *How to Plan and Lead All Age Worship*, Grove Books 2008

Leach, Chris: *Keeping our Kids*, Grove Books 2007

Leach, Chris & John: *And for your Children: leading children into the gifts and fruit of the Spirit*, Monarch 1994

Lenton, Sarah: *Creative Ideas for Children's Worship*, Canterbury Press 2012 May,

Scottie: *Children Matter: celebrating their place in the Church, family and community*, Eerdmans 2005

Melluish, Lindsay & Mark: *Family Time*, Kingsway 2002

Moore, Lucy: *All Age Worship*, BRF 2010

Moore, Lucy: *Messy Church*, BRF 2006

Moore, Lucy & Jane Leadbetter: *Starting Your Messy Church*, BRF 2012 Nye,

Rebecca: *Children's Spirituality – what it is and why it matters*, CHP 2009

Orme, Rona: *Rural Children, Rural Church – mission opportunities in the countryside*, CHP 2007

Palmer, Sue: *Toxic Childhood – how the modern world is damaging our children and what we can do about it*, Orion 2007

Richards, Anne & Peter Privett: *Through the Eyes of a Child – new insights in theology from a child's perspective*, CHP 2009

Stonehouse, Catherine: *Joining Children on a Spiritual Journey – nurturing a life of faith*, Baker Books 1998

Tripp, Tedd: *Shepherding a Child's Heart,* Shepherd Press 2009

Walters, David: *Kids in Combat – training children and youth to be powerful for God*, Creation House 2000

Withers, Margaret: *Mission-Shaped Children – moving towards a child-centred church*, CHP 2010

Withers, Margaret: *Not Just Sunday – setting up and running mid-week clubs for children*, CHP 2002

Websites
www.childtheology.org
Children – The Great Omission? vimeo.com/72329616

ReSource

ReSource is a registered Church of England charity based in Wells, Somerset. We work all over the UK and beyond, supporting local churches of all denominations and publishing a range of books and course materials to strengthen the mission and ministry of the Church, along with a termly full colour topical magazine.

Other ReSource publications by Roger Morgan include:

Decision - an explanation of what is involved in becoming a Christian. A short illustrated booklet which helps people to find a personal faith.

Beyond Ourselves - a course which explores the wider meaning of our lives. The first of a three-part discipleship programme *The God Who is There*. Designed for use with small groups of people who have no church background.

Beautiful Lives – sharing our faith with friends and neighbours. A group course which helps church members develop the confidence to share their faith naturally and effectively with others.

A Vision for your Church – outcomes of the Spirit
A booklet is designed to help a church identify its own unique and God-given vision.

If you would like to know more about our publications or about how ReSource can support the ministry of your church, or if you would like to get in touch with Roger, please do not hesitate to contact us.

Website: www.resource-arm.net
Email: office@resource-arm.net
Phone: 01749 672860